Hibernian

The Complete Story

The playing staff face the camera at the start of season 90-91.

Hibernian

The Complete Story

JOHN R. MACKAY

Foreword by

'THE PROCLAIMERS'

SPORTSPRINT PUBLISHING

EDINBURGH

ISBN 0 85976 321 8

Phototypeset by Newtext Composition Ltd., Glasgow.
Printed and bound by Bell & Bain Ltd., Glasgow.

Foreword

AS I WALKED INTO EASTER ROAD for the first time my dad turned to me and Craig to say " you'll enjoy this". 90 minutes later, Hibernian having scored 7 goals to St. Johnstone's 1, I really had to agree.

In recent years, as Hearts have added to their list of runner-up medals, it's been difficult persuading Edinburgh kids that following Hearts, when they could support Hibs, is like taking a Ford Escort because the Porsche you've been offered needs repairing. Mentioning the fact that Hibs were winning matches in Europe when Hearts were still trying to locate the car ferry, cuts no ice with bungalow bairns desperate to see silverware come to Edinburgh.

This book puts recent dramatic events into perspective. Hibs have often struggled, but the good times have made things worthwhile because our club has been associated with progressive ideas and skilful football and these things matter a great deal to Hibernian people.

Anyway, for those of us unavailable for the coming fixtures at Mercer Stadium it is, and will remain, **Hibernian Forever**!

Charlie Reid
(*THE PROCLAIMERS*)

Acknowledgements

MY THANKS go to the following for their help in the preparation of this book: John Anderson, Capital Press, Stuart Collie, Stewart Cowe, Tom Farmer, Great Scot International, Brian Hamilton, Sammy Kean, George Lister, Richard Raginia, Scotsman Publications plc, Raymond Sparkes, Philip Thomson and Iain Whyte.

The team picture on the back cover is reproduced by permission of Sportapic Sports Agency.

John R. Mackay

The photographs on the front cover are reproduced by courtesy of the Hibernian Match Day Magazine.

The team picture on the back cover is reproduced by permission of Sportapic Sports Agency.

Contents

PART ONE
Hibernian United

SUMMER 1990 was to be one that no Hibernian supporter will forget. It was the time of the famous – or notorious – bid by Wallace Mercer, Chairman of Hearts, to take over Hibernian. It would turn out to be an error of judgement because it didn't take history into account. The name of a great club would disappear, and with it all its proud traditions. As soon as the bid was announced on 4th June, hundreds of supporters gathered at Easter Road to voice their anger and concern.

What the bid had failed to foresee was the storm of emotion it would unleash, as letters in the local press revealed.

Kathleen Harvey, only surviving child of Michael Whelahan, one of the founders of Hibernian.

Very much in the front line of the take-over defence, David Duff (right) and Jim Gray (left).

"I really didn't realise until now just how much the club still means to me."

"Football is the supporters. Their passion, pride, memories, ideas, hopes, energy and emotion are the most important part of any football club."

Or this from the Western Australia Hibs Supporters' Club: "He (Wallace Mercer) should be reminded that not only is he destroying a very famous football club, but he's destroying history, Edinburgh history, a way of life for a lot of people."

Within hours of the bid Kenny McLean, a former Vice-Chairman of Hibernian, became chairman of a Hands Off Hibs committee. The campaign was to gain rapidly in strength. Ten thousand fans turned up at Easter Road on 9th June for a rally attended by former players – Pat Stanton, Joe Baker and Jimmy O'Rourke were there. Edinburgh District Council also entered the scene, offering to refurbish and provide Meadowbank Stadium as an alternative to Easter Road.

Financial counter-measures were being taken. The man who perhaps played the leading role in ensuring the continued independence of Hibernian was businessman Tom Farmer who, with his close associate Tom Harrison, bought a substantial shareholding. Vital also was the intervention of former Hibernian chairman Kenny Waugh who purchased a sizeable portion of shares.

At an Usher Hall rally on 2nd July both Tom Farmer and Kenny McLean were to receive standing ovations. And Chairman David Duff promised to stand firm and fight the bid.

The battle was over by 14th July. The bid had been withdrawn. Said Kenny McLean: "This is a Hibs victory and a real victory for the fans." Bill Alcorn, General Secretary of the Hibs Supporters' Association, said: "Tonight we all

Shocked fans gather outside Easter Road on 9th June, 1990.

have a sense of freedom." Said Pat Stanton: "The fans are the most important people in the game but in this instance they were disregarded. They have won because they refused to back down or be ignored."

Tom Farmer had this to say: "I am a Leither. I was born there, I grew up there and I played in the streets. I know what Hibernian mean to that community and to the city of Edinburgh. But we all have to recognise that drastic changes will have to be made in the way Hibs are run."

That last remark struck a new note, and one with significance for the future. The trading performance of Edinburgh Hibernian plc, the quoted company which own Hibernian Football Club, had made it vulnerable to takeover. The company was to emerge with a new board that would combine respect for the club with financial strength and skill. On it would be Tom Farmer and Tom Harrison. David Duff remained as a non-executive director, while at the football club itself Jim Gray became chief executive.

Businessman and accountant Alister Dow took over the executive chairmanship of Edinburgh Hibernian plc. Let the final words be his: "I see my job as welding the enthusiasm of the fans to the commercial expertise of people like myself." Once again the future of Hibernian looks good.

The Hands Off Hibs campaign in full swing visit Tynecastle to hand in a 50,000 signature petition opposing the takeover bid.

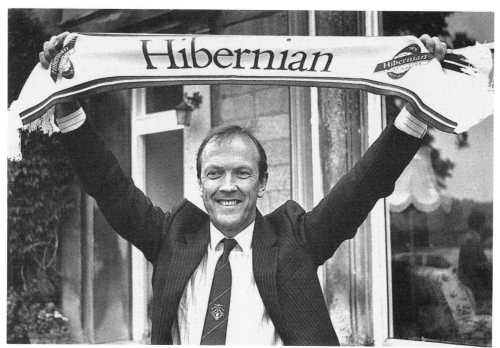

Alister Dow, Hibernian's new Chairman from 1st August, 1990.

PART TWO

The
Hibs Story

CHAPTER 1

The Old Hibs

IRISH SETTLERS have migrated to Scotland for centuries to escape hard times and harsh conditions on the Emerald Isle, but the community which clustered round St. Patrick's Church in Edinburgh's Cowgate in the 1870s were mostly first and second generation immigrants, closely knit and with a strong awareness of their roots. Just round the corner from the church was St. Mary's Street Hall, built in 1869 to provide a school for the local children and a clubroom for the Catholic Young Men's Society attached to St. Patrick's.

An early account of Hibernian Football Club relates how some members of this Society were watching the new-fangled game of Association Football being played in the East Meadows in the autumn of 1875 and were in little doubt that they could do at least as well. So they got the necessary approval of Canon Hannon at St. Patrick's and went ahead. A ball was bought, Michael Whelahan was elected captain, Malachy Byrne secretary, and on the captain's proposal, the new club was called Hibernian. The name left no misunderstanding about whom the club represented, and they were quickly joined by several other Irish youths who had been playing for a side called White Star. Pat Cavanagh, Frank Rourke and "Tailor" Flynn were among those who came from this source.

Some of the original rules of the club make strange reading today. Entry cost one shilling, with a monthly subscription of sixpence. Members missing the rollcall at 7.45 at the monthly meeting were fined twopence, and those who did not pay their fines were excluded from the distribution of surplus funds at the end of the season. Practices took place on Tuesdays, Thursdays and Saturdays at the Meadows – "regular attendance requested" – and anyone who has driven across the Meadows in December will appreciate that this called for some commitment!

Members also had to provide their own "uniform" – white guernsey with harp on the left breast, green and white knickerbockers, green cap and hose. The harp, with "Erin – go – Bragh", or "Ireland for Ever" in Gaelic, underneath, was adopted as the club crest.

Life had a difficult start for the new club. They applied to join the newly formed Edinburgh F.A., but were told to join the Scottish F.A. first. So they tried to join the S.F.A. but the national association, according to Tirconnell's account of 1887, "thus early displaying a spirit which has all along marked their dealings with the Hibernians, refused them admission".

The Hibs team of 1876 in their hooped strip of that time. Back row (l to r) Hall, Quinn, Gilhooley, Beveridge, Candlin, Rourke, Creamer and McGrath. Middle – Byrne, Donelly, Whelehan, Hughes, Browne and Keegan. Front – Meechan, Watson and Flynn.

Fortunately, the E.F.A. were more accommodating: they were trying to promote the game in the east, and recognised that Hibs "promised to be a useful acquisition for the district". Not only were Hibs admitted, but a petition was signed by all the capital's prominent players, so that when Hibs next tried to join the S.F.A. in 1876, they were successful. They were unable to take part in the 1876-77 Scottish Cup, but made their debut in the Edinburgh Cup.

Progress from that point was faster: in October 1876, Hibs' game with Swifts was included in *The Scotsman's* list of fixtures for the first time, and in February 1877, Hibs scored their first win over Heart of Midlothian.

By the end of the season, Hibs were recognised as a force in Edinburgh football – a heavy robust side which nevertheless dribbled and passed well, and mighty kickers. Mal Byrne and Frank Rourke were selected for the E.F.A. side which held the mighty Queens Park to a single goal in October, and Owen Quinn joined them against 3rd Lanark RV, the Third Lanark of later years, in December.

Hibs beat Hearts again in their first Scottish Cup tie, and sailed through the regional groupings to the national stages. There they met Thornliebank, a Renfrewshire side who reached the final a year or two later, and after two draws, both sides went through, after the rules of the time. Hibs next travelled to Govan to meet South Western in the 5th round, the first time an eastern club had gone so far, and won much respect although they lost 3-0.

There was little doubt that this run had helped kindle interest in the game in Edinburgh – rugby was already entrenched as the establishment game – but what really set it alight was the marathon Edinburgh Cup final which took place in the spring of 1878, and appropriately between Hibs and Hearts.

The Hibs team of around 1882 with the Edinburgh Cup and the Second XI Cup which they held outright, and the new East of Scotland Shield which replaced the former.

The Edinburgh Cup

THE MAIN VENUE FOR BIGGER GAMES IN EDINBURGH was Powburn, on the south side of the city. Powburn Toll straddled what is now Mayfield Road at the railway bridge, and the football ground occupied what is now West Savile Terrace and McDowell Road. It was there that Hibs met Hearts in their first final on February 9.

The game finished goalless, although Hibs had two scores disallowed, and a replay took place a week later. This one finished with a late equaliser by Hibs to make the score 1-1, and a general to-do when the Hearts' captain refused to play extra time. To avoid a repetition of the trouble, prices were raised for the third instalment, but after an hour there was a mass break-in of those who had been excluded on financial grounds. They had missed both goals in another 1-1 draw.

The Hibs team of about 1880, believed to be photographed at Mayfield. Pat Cavanagh is the player holding the ball by the lace.

For the fourth game there was a change of venue, to Bainfield at Merchiston; this turned out to be the roughest yet, and yet another 1-1 draw, after half an hour's extra time. And so it was finally back to Powburn, where, on April 20, nine weeks after the initial engagement there, Hearts won somewhat against the run of play by the odd goal in five.

Hibs' revenge was quick and ample, and a year later the Irish supporters were celebrating all the way back in the special trains from Corstorphine where their favourites had taken the trophy from Hearts by 2-0. A year after that Hibs beat Dunfermline in a somewhat one-sided final, so that by 1880-81 they were poised for the hat-trick which would give them the cup to keep.

Hearts of course were determined to prevent this happening – firstly by proposing that Hibs should be made to resign from the E.F.A. because of the physical style of their play and the uncivilised behaviour of their followers. The Irish were still not the city's most popular minority, and Hibs escaped on a tied vote. Hearts were next unable to prevent Hibs' progress on the field, but, clutching at straws now, they complained that the 3-1 score in the press should only have been 2-1.

So Hibs progressed to beat St. Bernard's and take the cup back to St.

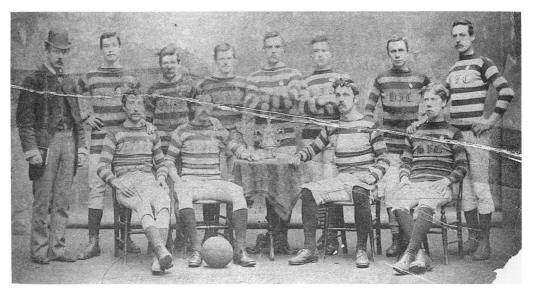

Hibs' first success – winners of the 1879 Edinburgh Cup. Michael Whelehan is the stern looking individual with his hand on the table, and the ball at his feet.

Patrick's. The E.F.A. replaced it with a shield, with crests top and bottom, and with interest in it now extending far outside the city boundary, it was named the East of Scotland Shield.

Hibs' success in the competition, however, was unabated – following their defeat at Powburn, they were undefeated in it for ten years, despite entries which grew to more than sixty teams. They won the Shield every year to 1887, except one, and beat Hearts in the competition in every one of these years. The exception was in 1885, when Hibs scratched in the final because of a squabble over dates, and the trophy went to University, who had beaten Hearts in the semi-finals.

On The Move

WITH SUCH AN EXPANSION OF THE GAME, Hibs had long since moved from the Meadows, first of all to Powderhall in 1878, where they took part in an early floodlighting experiment in October of that year; they also took part in a notable Scottish Cup tie against Helensburgh, in which the goal which would probably have won the game for Hibs was disallowed – because a Hibs' player put the ball between the posts when the keeper was out of his goal!

By the following season they had moved again, to Mayfield, and had changed their colours too – to plain green jerseys. Mayfield was the same venue as was previously known as Powburn, and had been renamed as the old village was demolished to make way for Mayfield Road. It could not have been very convenient for the players, because the changing rooms were still in St. Mary's Street. The new ground was to have been opened by Rangers, but the Glasgow club were unable to raise a team, and Kilmarnock Athletic did the honours a week later.

Hibs did not stay long on the south side of the city, however, and in early 1880 they moved back across town to Easter Road, not the present site, but across the railway footbridge to the south, where Bothwell Street now stands. In the summer, came the first round of personnel changes – Willie Donnelly, one of the founder members, left the area, and Michael Whelahan stood down as captain in favour of Pat Cavanagh.

Hibs were happy at Easter Road, close to their support, and with its enthusiastic backing became almost invincible on their own patch. It is true that Hearts won there in the 1880-81 Scottish Cup, but that was the only time in ten years that Hibs did not reach the all-in stages. A year later, the first grandstand was built at what was now clearly seen as a permanent home, and in 1881-82, no fewer than nine Hibs men were involved in E.F.A. representative games – Cox, Byrne, Flynn, Rourke, McKernan, McFadyen, Cavanagh, Waugh and O'Brien.

A period of consolidation followed, and by Hibs' standards 1882-83 was unexciting. It was also a time of transition, because Frank Rourke had emigrated, and Cox and McKernan had become the first of many Hibs to go after richer pickings south of the border. But the lull only lasted the one season, because Hibs made a major signing coup in the following summer.

Sunday School Picnic

IT HAPPENED THAT a St. Patrick's church outing ended up in Ayrshire, and as part of the entertainment a scratch Hibs team took on a local eleven. It was not the picnic that might have been expected, and the outcome was that three of the Ayrshire players were recruited to play for Hibs. They were Pat McGinn, a strapping defender, Jim McGhee, the next captain of the club and the first Hibs' player to play for his country, and James McLaren, a crafty midfielder who would have been the first Hibs' man to be capped, according to the president of the E.F.A. a year or two later, had it been known whether it was Scotland or Ireland he was eligible for.

The anti-Irish lobby was immediately re-energised, and the E.F.A. persuaded to ban these players from competitions under its jurisdiction because they were

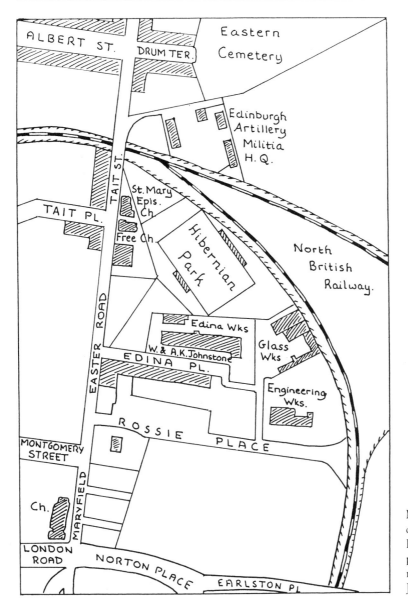

Map showing the position of the first Easter Road Park, drawn from a map published in 1888 by near neighbours W. & A. K. Johnstone.

not "local". The ban was ratified twice before the Irish supporters stage-managed a situation whereby the arguments went back and forth all night, apparently boring all present to distraction, until when at one point enough of their opponents were out of the room for a refreshment, the argument collapsed, a vote was required, and the Ayrshire men were declared eligible. In any case, the same Edinburgh F.A. had already selected McGhee and McLaren for its representative side!

With this threesome, Hibs were now better equipped to challenge for national honours, and reached their first Scottish Cup semi-final in 1884, again the first eastern side to do so. Semi-finals were still not played on neutral ground, but despite having home advantage, Hibs were outgunned by a bigger and more experienced Queens Park team, and went down by 5-1.

By now, the parochial squabbles about local players had been submerged in the bigger argument about professionalism. The argument seemed to be that to pay players would favour the bigger city clubs at the expense of the others, quite apart from the amateur ethics involved, and those who opposed payments on moral grounds. On the other hand, to remain amateur would only increase the drain of top players going to England, where professionalism had recently been approved.

The Scottish clubs voted to remain amateur, although it seems that yet again Hibs and Hearts had different opinions, because within months, the Tynecastle side were expelled for paying players for a cup-tie against Dunfermline.

Hibs on the other hand continued to be the east's main challengers for the Scottish Cup, and they reached the semi-finals again in 1885. This time their opponents were Renton, the most illustrious of the village sides which were such a feature of early Scottish football, but although they had ground advantage again, Hibs were unable to profit from it, and Renton won an exciting struggle by 3-2.

A year further, and Hibs had added that precocious teenager Willie Groves to their staff, and had reached yet another Scottish Cup semi-final, and again against Renton. Again they were favoured with a home draw and again were unable to make that advantage count. In blinding snow, the "Rantin" notched up two quick goals, and try as they might, Hibs were unable to make any impression.

If nothing else, it was therefore a more experienced Hibs team which embarked on the trail to Hampden in 1886-87. In reaching the semi-final yet again, they accounted for Durhamtown Rangers, Hearts, Mossend Swifts, Third Lanark and Cambuslang. Mossend Swifts, in the middle of an amazing run of only one defeat in eight years in front of their own partisan fans, gave them most trouble, and Hibs were more than a little relieved to earn a draw at West Calder, while the outstanding result was the Christmas Day 2-1 win against Third Lanark on a frozen Cathkin Park.

The 1887 semi-final was against Vale of Leven, and for the fourth time, Hibs were drawn at home. Both teams underwent special training, and a huge crowd turned out to see Hibs finally make it with a 3-1 win. Unfortunately the celebrations came to a halt when it became known that the Vale were protesting that Willie Groves had been given cash by Hibs. No further evidence was offered, but the meeting to discuss the protest was amazingly held over until after the final between Hibs and Dumbarton.

The story of the final is told elsewhere in this book (see Matches to

Remember), but Hibs won 2-1 to bring the trophy to Edinburgh for the first time. The following week the protest from Vale of Leven was discussed. The only evidence was the hearsay of one employee at Groves' place of work, but such was the bias of the committee that it still required the casting vote of the chairman to clear Hibs and let them keep the cup.

For the remainder of that season and into the next, Hibs continued to play many games for Catholic charities, and although the general impression was that their form had shaded a little since their Hampden triumph, they did challenge Preston North End for the Association Football Championship of the World – and beat them too (see Matches to Remember). Their success and philanthropy, however, had already sown the seeds of their undoing, and the writing was on the wall – literally – before 1887 was out.

Brother Walfrid, a Marist priest from Glasgow, had been impressed not only by the Hibs' performances but by the gate receipts therefrom, and was responsible for a handbill in late 1887 to launch Celtic. The aims were twofold – to supply "funds for the maintenance of the 'dinner tables' of the needy children", and to select "a team which will do credit to the Catholics of the West of Scotland as the Hibernians have been doing in the East".

It is the job of Celtic historians to explain why they failed in the first of these; the uncharitable methods of securing the second destroyed Hibs. On May 8th, with misplaced kindness, Hibs played Cowlairs in a match to open Celtic's new ground at Janefield. When they returned there to open the following season against their hosts, the results of Celtic's recruitment were plain for all to see. McKeowan, Gallagher, Groves, McLaren and Coleman of the previous year's Hibs were all in Celtic colours, and more were to defect west. There was no proof of financial skullduggery, but few in Edinburgh believed that the integrity of the new club remained intact.

The Hibs' supporters, for example, were in no doubt and made a threatening audience for Celtic's first visit to Edinburgh, surrounding the Glasgow players on several occasions before the proceedings were brought to an early halt to give the Celtic team the element of surprise to enable them to reach their train. The East of Scotland F.A. President, speaking at the Hearts' annual concert of all places, said that everyone deplored what had happened to Hibs, and that "better things might have been expected from the club" which had caused it.

Hibs' problems quickly mounted. Two more players had left for England, and they were dismissed from the two major tournaments at the first time of asking by Mossend Swifts and new neighbours Leith Athletic. Their crowds now numbered just a few hundreds of their closest followers, and on occasion Hibs had to recruit from amongst them to field a team. They were threatened with expulsion from their ground because of the continuing expansion of the city, and tried unsuccessfully to get the lease of St. Bernards' Logie Green transferred to them.

Even Celtic, with perhaps an element of conscience, played Hibs to raise funds to keep them going, and Leith Athletic did likewise "for their once formidable opponents". But by the autumn the end was in sight. They had been told to leave Easter Road, and their final game was a Scottish Cup tie against old rivals Dumbarton. This proved to be the final straw; the loyal captain, Jim McGhee, and only survivor of the good days, gave away the first goal and Dumbarton won 9-1. With a scratch team and no ground, it was now just a matter of time, and what was expected to be Σthe last appearance of the Hibernians came on February 14, 1891, when Leith Athletic beat them 6-1 at Bank Park.

A recently discovered photograph entitled 'Ye Olde Hibs 1887'. Back row (l to r) T. Maley, J. McGhee, Mr McFadyen (secy), P. McGinn, P. McGovern, P. Clark. Middle row – R. McGeachan (asst. secy), Lee, Tobin, J. McLaren, O. Brannigan, W. Groves. Front row – J. Lundie, G. Smith, A. McMahon.

CHAPTER 2

Hibs Mark Two

FORTUNATELY, not everyone took a pessimistic view. One group tried to continue as Leith Hibernians, based at Hawkhill, but Leith Hibs managed only one game there and did not survive the summer break.

But behind the scenes, efforts were ongoing. A meeting of those "favourable to the resuscitation of the (Hibernian Football) Club" was held in Buchanan's Hotel in the High Street on March 7th, 1892. The eleven who attended were Messrs. Mitchell, Smith, O'Brien, Farmer, McCabe, McPhee, Rafferty, Connolly, Bennett, Docherty and Sandilands, and they contributed the first £25 to a guarantee fund.

In the next few weeks, likely donors and guarantors were circularised, and a quest was initiated for a suitable ground. Mr. Lapsley, the proprietor of Powderhall, was sympathetic, but his park was only available from November to February. A tip from an S.F.A. member that Logie Green might be vacant come the new season proved fruitless, but Councillor Hunter offered his services to negotiate on the club's behalf with the Trinity Hospital Trust to secure a ground at Easter Road.

It was hoped it would be ready for season 1892-93, but that proved impossible, and a further meeting was told that that was because it had proved harder to attract financial backing than had been anticipated. But it was decided to go ahead and a public meeting took place in St. Mary Street Hall in late October. Charlie Sandilands was called to the chair, and he explained that no contact had been made, or was intended, with the old committee. It was also stressed that the resuscitated club would be run on non-sectarian lines, although about six months later, it was agreed that Irish youths would have precedence over young men of "any other nationality".

Hibs were therefore back in business, and the first meeting of the club was held on December 12th. It was agreed to elect five office bearers and twelve committee members; Nicholas Burke was president, Thomas Flood vice-president, although not without opposition because he was a member of Celtic, Charlie Sandilands secretary, C.F. Perry match secretary, and Philip Farmer treasurer.

There was much to be discussed, and, with a committee of seventeen and several sub-committees, much discussion. The club colours would be green jerseys and blue knickers; Begson and McIntosh, joiners, were engaged to bring the

John Farmer (right) new president of the club and widely forecast to do well for it, and Dan McMichael (left) secretary and manager 1903–19, were featured in the Evening Dispatch in 1911.

The official stamp of Hibernian FC following resuscitation in 1892, taken from the Secretary's minute book of the time.

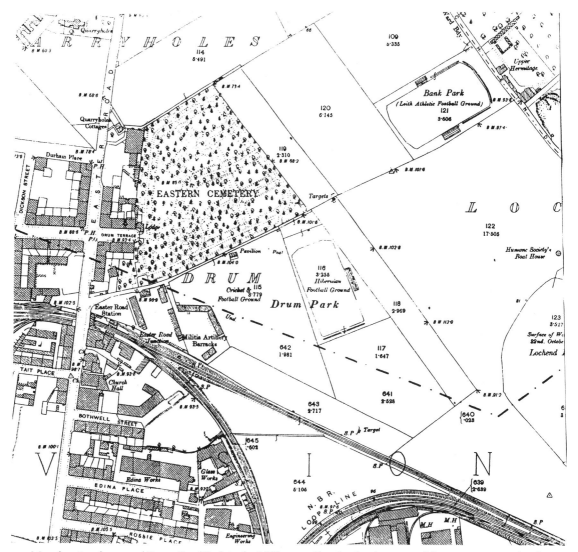

Map showing the second Easter Road Park in the 1890s, as well as the development of the previous ground and the proximity of Leith Athletic's Bank Park. The only access was by the footpath alongside the Eastern Cemetery.

ground up to scratch. There was a discussion whether the stand should be high enough to let those in it see over those standing in front, and a sub-committee voted 6-5 to let the pitch to a local butcher for grazing. This was some time before they voted to buy a ball!

That did not happen until a few days before the first game. Hearts had agreed to open the new Easter Road on February 4th, but a cup-tie against Polton Vale took precedence, and Clyde did the honours, for a £15 guarantee. Not only a ball, but two pails, two baths, twelve basins, two tankards, two looking glasses and four combs were acquired to bring the facilities up to scratch. They had also assembled a fair group of players, including Paddy Murray and Peter Meechan who later played for Scotland, and a 4-3 defeat from their league opponents was considered a satisfactory start.

The Second Division

BY THE END OF THE SEASON, the new side had won as many games as they had lost, and had recorded wins over Dumbarton, St. Mirren and Leith of the league sides. With a committee of seventeen involved, team selection was a protracted process, and there was clearly room for improvement: "the Secretary moved that we look for another goalkeeper, as Cox was not class for the team". There was debate as to whether to let out the ball after matches, and a deputation was sent to visit the editor of the *Evening News* to complain about "the unfair and biased criticism of our team which appears in their columns from time to time".

The question of professionalism took up many a long hour, and there was also that of league status, when Hibs were one of the sides approached by Airdrieonians, who were instrumental in forming a second division. Hibs thereby became founder members, and their negotiator, Mr. Flood, became the league's treasurer. A big effort was put in to enhance the ground, and the massive expenditure of £150 meant that they could not afford goal nets as well. Hibs' first league campaign started with a 2-1 win over Northern in Glasgow, and ended with a 10-1 rout of Port Glasgow Athletic.

They finished two points ahead of Cowlairs who were second, and a green championship flag, with yellow harp but no crown, was duly ordered. In addition, Hibs had won nine and drawn three of seventeen games against First Division clubs, and were clearly the best-equipped side to play in that company. Unfortunately, promotion was in the hands of the league clubs, and Hibs and Cowlairs were left out in favour of Clyde. At Easter Road there was outrage at this, and in particular at the manner in which a couple of the clubs concerned had selfishly organised a lobby to keep Hibs out.

Hibs' target for 1895 was therefore to win another Second Division flag, and this they achieved with consummate ease – they finished eight points clear after the eighteen-game programme, and scored 90 goals in the process. This time their claim for top league status was irresistible, and they were admitted to the First Division. During the season, the Scottish Cup draw had done what Hibs' match secretaries had failed to, and brought Celtic to Easter Road. Given the bitterness felt in Edinburgh about the Glasgow club's attitude in 1887 and 1894,

HIBERNIAN F
·1894

C. F. Perry
President

SCOTTISH CUP 1887
EDINBURGH CUP 1894
ROSEBERY CUP 1894

T. L. McFarlan

T. Gillule
Hon. Vice President

B. Breslin
Captain

A. Nowie

W. Smith

C. Sandilands
Secretary

· SECOND ·
LEAGUE CHAMPIONS
· 1893 - 94. ·
· 1894 - 95. ·

there was a certain atmosphere surrounding the game, and a huge crowd of 15,000 in special stands were delirious over Hibs' 2-0 win.

The ill-feeling about Celtic was increased further when it became known that the Parkhead club had made a protest regarding the appearance of a Hibs' player for a junior side during the previous summer, and had been awarded a replay. A much smaller attendance jeered and booed while Celtic won that, also by 2-0.

The Logie Green Final

IT WAS IN AUGUST 1895 that Willie Groves came back to Hibs from England to an emotional homecoming, but, although only in his mid-twenties, his health was beginning to fail. The old skills were still there, though, and Hibs went on to finish third in the table, as well as beating Rangers on the way to their second Scottish Cup final. Their opponents were Hearts, and, with common sense dictating, the final took place at St. Bernards' Logie Green ground. A fear of crushing restricted the crowd to only 16,000; Hibs failed to recapture the form which had taken them so far, and Hearts were well worth their 3-1 win.

Hibs had come a long way, and the following season they finished second in the table, and with a 100% home record, the only time they have achieved that

THE LEAGUE RACE.

The above illustration gives the positions of the First Division League Clubs up to, but not including, to-day.

Edinburgh sides dominated the 1895–1896 League Championship race, as this illustration from the 'Evening Times' shows.

feat. International recognition came first to Bobby Neil in 1896, and the following year, Kennedy, Murray and wing-half Breslin played together against Wales. During the five seasons to 1901, Hibs, along with Hearts and the Old Firm, comprised the top four in the league, but it was nevertheless a period of transition; Martin had to give the game up through injury, Neil went to Rangers, and Jimmy McGeachan, rated by some as the best centre-half in the country, went to England.

On the credit side, there were bright youngsters in John Price, a free-scoring forward, and Dougal on the flank, along with Alec Raisbeck, who won several caps later in his career at Liverpool. Martin's replacement was Hamilton Handling, who like his predecessor could play in attack or defence, and Paddy Callaghan from Jordanhill started a long career at Easter Road in February 1899. Bob Glen, captain of Renton's 1895 cupwinning eleven, brought experience to the defence, and the young goalkeeper McCall played in the international trials.

There was also Willie McCartney, a powerful winger who had come from Leith, and Bobby Atherton, who won several Welsh caps, but the real signing scoop, in August 1900, was Harry Rennie, the extraordinarily extrovert goalkeeper

The Hibs' team which reached the 1896 Scottish Cup Final at Logie Green. Captain Bernie Breslin is holding the ball and goal scorer O'Neill is front, far right.

who had already been capped while with Hearts. Hibs already knew all about Rennie – Hearts and Hibs had met eleven times in 1899-1900 alone – and when his transfer to Celtic hit a snag, and Rennie was temporarily a free agent, they nipped in with a lucrative contract, much to the chagrin of the Tynecastle club.

Season 1901-02 turned out to be the one in which Hibs broke through again, but it did not start off looking that way in the league championship which, with only ten sides, was generally more or less over by Christmas. Given their problems of a few years earlier, Hibs did not want to be involved in applying for re-election, and they only missed that by the narrowest of margins, finishing sixth.

Year Of The Double

THE SECOND HALF WAS ALTOGETHER MORE ENCOURAGING, as Hibs swept through to another cup final. Queens Park were hammered 7-1 in Glasgow, and although Divers, a recruit from Celtic, missed a penalty and McCartney broke a leg, Hibs beat Rangers in the semi-finals at Ibrox more easily than the score might suggest. If it seemed unfortunate that the final – against Celtic - should be played at Parkhead, Hibs did not let it upset them, and they took the trophy for the second time by the only goal (see Matches to Remember). For good measure they took the Glasgow Charity Cup as well, trouncing Celtic 6-2 after being 5-0 ahead at the break.

For the remainder of the year, Hibs delivered everything they had promised. The league championship of 1902-03 was virtually over in October, when Hibs, with twenty-one points, were eight ahead of Rangers, Celtic, Hearts and Dundee. They scored five for the only time at Ibrox, and recorded their biggest win, 4-0, at Parkhead. Their league double over the Ibrox team was their last until 1964-65. When the formalities had been completed, Dundee had won the race for the also-rans, finishing six points adrift, and Hibs had lost only once, at Cathkin against Third Lanark.

As has so often been the case, the Hibs' joy was unrestrained – and short-lived. It was not long before the team was broken up by the lure of richer pickings: Andy McGeechan, scorer of the cupwinning goal, went to Bradford, Breslin finished his career with Celtic, Robertson went to Manchester United and Atherton to Middlesbrough. Within no time, Hibs were an average league side, and in fact in 1903-04, they finished fifth bottom in a league extended now to 14 clubs. It was as well for them that the First Division quickly expanded to 18 teams, because the longer card meant that clubs were not as dependant on a good cup run to make the second half of the season meaningful. For the rest of the decade, Hibs only reached one more semi-final.

It is not often that Hibs have held both the Scottish Cup and the League Championship. Early in 1903 they did, along with the Glasgow Charity Cup, the Rosebery Cup and the Macrae Cup, and the successful committee and playing staff as pictured above were:
Back (l to r) – P. Cannon, C. Carolan, P. Smith, A. McPhee, O. Brannigan, D. McMichael, F. Rennie, B. Lester, J. Pollock and Mr. Brandon.
Second back – J. Buchan, J. Hogg, A. Gray, R. Glen, H. Handling and J. Divers.
Second front – J. Stewart, B. Breslin, J. Harrower, R. Atherton, A. Robertson, J. McColl and H. G. Rennie.
Front – P. Callaghan and W. McCartney.

The problem again was the lack of a reserve team, especially at a time when a steady flow of players was attracted south. George Stewart replaced the unlucky McCartney on the right wing, then moved to the left to accommodate John Campbell, an Anglo-Scot from West Ham: soon after winning his first cap, Stewart moved to Manchester City. McConnochie replaced Buchan at centre-half, then joined Everton. Goalscoring was a chronic problem, but of all those tried, only Dick Harker, from Crystal Palace, proved a success, and he went to Hearts after a year or two.

Hibs' difficulties in regaining their former status continued. They recognised that their strange sloping pitch was not exactly ideal, and most of the club's resources during the first ten years of the century were directed towards their new stadium at Piershill. It was built on the most modern lines, with a cycle track to enable its use in summer, and was to accommodate fifty thousand fans.

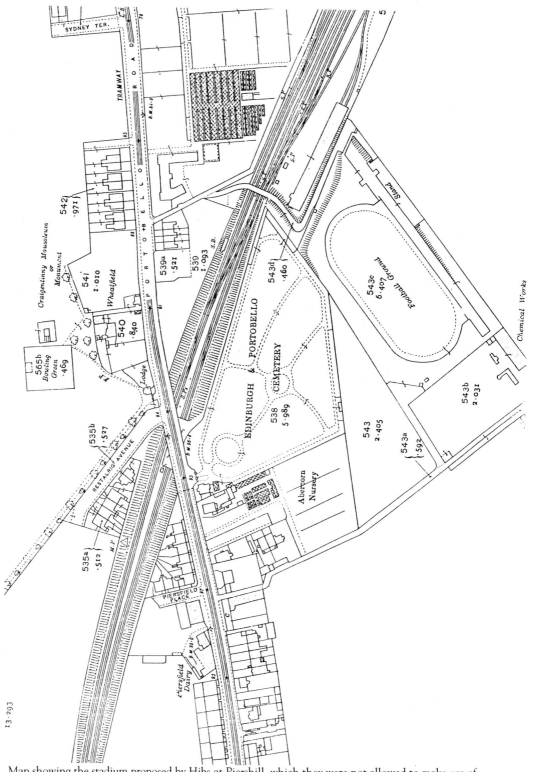

Map showing the stadium proposed by Hibs at Piershill, which they were not allowed to make use of. Portobello at the time was not part of Edinburgh.

An enamel badge struck to celebrate Hibs' Scottish Cup success in 1902.

Unfortunately, at the eleventh hour, the North British Railway Co. obtained a court order against them, on the grounds that they required one corner of Hibs' ground for a railway link. It was never built, but it deprived Hibs of the stadium, and threw them back on an increasingly rundown Easter Road.

Hibs were maybe still only an average side in first division terms, but they had their admirers – notably the Irish community in Dundee, who formed Dundee Hibernians in 1909 to emulate the Edinburgh ones. Hibs hanselled the new club's park, Tannadice, in August 1909, and as both clubs' colours were green, Hibs had to borrow Leith Athletic's black and white hoops for the occasion. Dundee Hibs went on to get league status, and are known now of course as Dundee United.

Although their league results did not totally reflect it, things were improving,

Bobby Atherton, capped nine times for Wales. A versatile player, he appeared for Hibs at wing-half, inside forward and on the wing. A captain of Hibs, he also captained Middlesbrough after leaving Easter Road. He was one of the first players to make football a full-time career. He was drowned during the 1914–18 war.

James Main, Hibs' brilliant right back, who was capped before his tragic death at 23 years of age.

and Hibs were finally putting together a fair side in the years before the war. Two 1908 signings who were to give sterling service were Matt Paterson, a rugged centre-half who was also the club's top scorer in 1910-11, and Willie Smith, a winger later capped by the league, and possessed of an accurate line in crosses. Harry Rennie, now a veteran, went to Rangers, but Hibs brought Willie Allan, another sound goalkeeper, from Falkirk.

Their plans suffered a tragic blow on Christmas Day 1909, when the brilliant young international full-back James Main was carried off at Firhill, and died of internal injuries a few days later. His replacement was Peter Kerr, a fine youngster from East Lothian who was to spend virtually his whole career with Hibs, but it was only with some difficulty that he was signed – his mother chased the Hibs' representative down the street when she heard why her son's services were required!

Goalscoring remained the main problem – Peggie from East Fife was the nearest thing to a solution to the problem until Hibs signed Jimmy Hendren from Cowdenbeath in early 1912. Hendren scored fifty league goals in three seasons, far in excess of his predecessors. With other forwards like the unorthodox Sam Fleming, Harry Anderson, later capped with Raith Rovers, and Smith, Hibs were better equipped up front than for many years, and they reached the 1914 cup final, beating Rangers on the way.

The opponents were Celtic and the venue Ibrox. Hibs played their part in an even game, and almost stole it when Smith missed a sitter in the final phase, with only the goalkeeper to beat. It was a miss which haunted Smith for the rest of his days, and Hibs regretted it in the replay the following Thursday – they were caught cold by two quick goals by the youthful Jimmy McColl, introduced by Celtic to provide sharpness up front. Smith did score late on for Hibs, but by then Celtic were four goals in front.

World At War

IT WAS IN 1914 that Archduke Ferdinand of Austria was murdered in Serbia and Europe went to war. It was expected to be a swift affair, but as time passed, more and more men were committed to the fray. In the first winter, a million men were in uniform, and during 1915, a further two million answered the call to enlist. Still this was not enough, and in early 1916, conscription was introduced. A year later women were moved into many jobs previously considered suitable only for men, and the previous incumbents were also shipped across the Channel. In 1918, those in charge were told that that summer's offensive had to succeed, because there was no-one else to send. Running a football team back home became harder and harder.

Meanwhile, the Scottish League continued, although, oddly, the Scottish Cup was cancelled in case the ties interfered with recruitment. Hibs' performance has to be taken in the context of the lack of manpower, and the disproportionate effect that it had on the clubs in the east of Scotland, where there were far fewer reserved occupations, which gave exemption from conscription, than in the industrial west. In 1914-15 Hibs finished a respectable eleventh, but for the rest of the war were never out of the bottom four.

It was in 1915 that the Second Division ceased, to be replaced by an Eastern League and a Western one. Within a year, the Eastern League had shrunk to ten clubs, and these included Dundee and Raith Rovers, who had

W. Allan, goal.

R. Wilson, outside-right.

S. Fleming, inside right.

N. Girdwood, right back.

R. Templeton, left back.

R. Kerr, right half-back.

Playing for Hibs at the time of the First World War. Bobby Templeton was later manager.

withdrawn from the Scottish League along with Aberdeen, with no guarantee of readmission. Only Armadale remained of the sides south of the Forth. In 1917-18, the Eastern League disappeared altogether, and Hibs and Hearts were left as the only two survivors of the seventeen east clubs who had been in action three years earlier.

Willie Allan saves from Owens of Celtic during the 1914 Scottish Cup Final. Templeton is on the right.

There seems little doubt that Hibs, bottom of the table by seven points and in serious financial trouble by 1918, would have been the next to go, and that they had not done so already was the result of the untiring efforts of manager and secretary Dan McMichael, the former professional runner who had been doing everything but playing during the latter period. He may even have considered that, with the shortage of players which once saw Peter Kerr keep goal at Ibrox, and full back Bobby Templeton quite frequently deputise between the posts.

Hibs used thirty-five players in that grim season, and a lightweight and makeshift side came in for some heavy punishment, losing seven at Kilmarnock and nine at Greenock in a mudbath, but McMichael kept their heads above water until he died during the flu epidemic of 1919.

Hibs players at Gullane prepare for the 1914 Cup Final.

A. Gray, P. Boyle, R. Glen, J. Hogg, D. McMichael (Secretary), P. Smith (Treasurer), F. Docherty (Vice-President), R. Atherton, P. Callaghan, J. Harrower, H. Rennie, H. Handling, Wm. McCartney, A. Robertson (Captain). The Hibs team around the turn of the Century.

CHAPTER 3

Between The Wars

FROM THE POSITION in which Hibs found themselves in 1919, things could only get better. The first improvement was a run to the semi-finals of the Victory Cup, with home ties until their defeat by St. Mirren at Tynecastle. The income from this run bought a much-needed set of new strips – the old jerseys had become completely discoloured and had been the butt of some jokes in the press, especially in the west. Also, Davy Gordon, who had come from Hull as a player during the war, was appointed manager, and a serious recruitment drive started.

The early post-war period was a transitional one all round. The league was extended to 22 clubs to take back those who had folded during hostilities, for two years until automatic promotion and relegation were introduced. Clubs had to combine their pre-war players back from the continent with their signings since.

Despite Hibs' wartime difficulties, only Peter Kerr of their 1914 team was to feature in the '20s, although Bobby Templeton remained as a utility player. Matt Paterson returned too, but after a couple of years injury persuaded him to step down in favour of Willie Miller, signed as an inside forward. With Hugh Shaw, another teenager signed late in the war as a forward, turning into a top-class wing half, and the fine young partnership of McGinnigle and Dornan settling in at the back, Hibs had the making of a stable defence. In goal, Hibs' problems had been solved when Barney Lester spotted Willie Harper, a big strong blacksmith playing for Edinburgh Emmet.

Up front, two junior inside men came from Glasgow – Jimmy Dunn from the St. Anthony's that was so prolific a nursery for Celtic, and Johnny Halligan from Shawfield Juniors. When "Darkie" Walker signed from Rob Roy to take the left-wing berth, Harry Ritchie, a big bustling winger who was becoming popular with Hibs on the left, switched to the right where he struck up a notable partnership with Dunn. That really only left the no. 9 shirt to be successfully filled. The solution this time turned out to be an old adversary, Jimmy McColl, who had scored against Hibs in the 1914 cup final, and was now playing with Stoke.

It was not long before this transformation in personnel was reflected on the pitch. Even in the first post-war season, Hibs cruised along in the top half of the table, until a traumatic cup defeat at Armadale affected their league form too and

Willie Miller, Hibs' leading scorer in 1917–18.
He later developed into a fine centre-half.

(Players) – Dornan, Shaw, Harper, Miller, Ritchie, McColl, Kerr, Walker, McGinnigle, Halligan and Dunn.
(This is the famous Hibs' team that reached the Scottish Cup final in 1923 and 1924 and lost on each occasion.)

they finished five from the bottom. Despite that, it was for their cup exploits that the Hibs' team of the early '20s became noted, and they reached the 1923 final. By now, Harper was recognised as Scotland's top goalkeeper, so it was all the more galling that a single mistake by him should enable Cassidy to score the only goal for Celtic.

A year later came another chance, with Hibs reaching the final again, this time at Ibrox against Airdrie, at the time a top side with players like Hughie Gallagher and Bob McPhail. Again the fates were not with Hibs. Sentiment had come into the team selection, because Dunn was not fully fit, but the same eleven turned out as had the previous year. Dunn and Ritchie soon had to swap places, Airdrie scored twice in the first quarter of the game, and a lopsided Hibs' attack never looked like pulling them back.

Alex Maley, brother of the Celtic manager, had taken over managerial duties, with Davy Gordon going to St. Bernards. Maley was not universally popular at Easter Road because of his family connections with Celtic, and in particular because of his being directly related to some of the 1888 defectors. He is often given the credit for the team which his predecessor had built, when in fact it was during his time there that one of the more damaging decisions was taken regarding the club – to scrap the reserve team. Hibs finished third in the 1925 league championship – their best for many years before or after – but early in 1925-26, Maley resigned, to be replaced by the veteran defender, Bobby

How 'Evening News' cartoonist Tom Curr saw Hibs' defeat by Airdrie in the 1924 cup final.

Jimmy McColl died in 1978 at 85 years of age. The grand old man of Easter Road was a member of the great Hibs' team of the 20's. He was the trainer to three championship winning teams.

Templeton. This seems to have upset Peter Kerr, who had wanted the job, and he went briefly to Hearts.

Meanwhile, Hibs' search for better premises had continued fruitlessly, but by 1924 they had negotiated a 25-year lease for Easter Road, and set about renovating the ground as a permanent home. The slope, which had given the pitch such a peculiar aspect, was largely levelled out, and the pitch moved sideways for about forty yards. The present stand was erected, on the opposite side from where the "eggbox" had stood, with changing facilities underneath, rather than in a separate pavilion as was the custom at the time. Entrances, exits and all the usual additional work brought the total cost up to no less than £20,000.

Unfortunately, a building strike held up completion, and Hibs had to play a couple of home games at Tynecastle on Friday nights, before Queens Park hanselled the new ground in September 1924.

Under Bobby Templeton, things went downhill quite quickly, although little blame was put on the new manager; an appalling injury list was exacerbated by the lack of reserve strength; and Willie Harper went to Arsenal. Harper had been turning out for Hibs even when quite lame, because they did not have another goalkeeper on the staff, so his departure left something of a problem. The Scottish national team were having a purple passage in their jousts with England, and this resulted in most of them going south. The goalkeeping situation was not resolved satisfactorily for some time, until Hibs signed Willie Robb from Rangers, in exchange for Hugh Shaw. An internationalist now past thirty, Robb was to gain further honours with Hibs, and was renowned for the outsize caps which characterised his appearance.

By the spring of 1926, Hibs were far down the table, and had to go to Clydebank to play what was in effect their first relegation battle. They won it by

Hugh Shaw   Jimmy McColl   Harry Ritchie

1-0, Shaw the scorer, and for the following two years they had a respectable mid-table position. The attack had not changed, although McColl was by now a veteran, and all five members of it hit double figures in goals in 1926-27; a year later, Hibs reached the Scottish Cup semis – a remarkable game inasmuch as Rangers played at neutral Tynecastle – and first McColl and then Dunn became the first players to score a hundred competitive goals for Hibs. Jimmy Dunn also gained footballing immortality by playing for the "Wembley Wizards" XI which thrashed England 5-1 in March 1928.

Ritchie and Dunn joined Everton in the summer of 1928, and Hibs' decline gathered momentum. The replacements were Murray, an aging utility player, and Finlay who had come from Dundee United but had made little impact. The fullbacks McGinnigle and Dornan were also of veteran status, though after transition another fine partnership, of Hector Wilkinson and Duncan Urquhart, took over. Miller and McColl appeared less and less, the latter usually as a stopgap winger, and the centre-forward position caused as much concern as any. Eddie Gilfeather and Willie Dick came from Airdrie and Celtic to bolster the defence, but Hibs slumped to 14th in 1929 and 17th a year later.

The problems were not confined to their performances on the field either. The economic slump and depression which followed it brought many clubs to the verge of bankruptcy, and pushed some beyond. Hibs' problems were compounded because of their ground improvements in 1924. These had been financed by means of debenture, and the debenture holders were unhappy about the lower security of their investment caused by the financial insecurity of the club. They fought for – and got – a say in the running of the club.

Although Hibs had been a non-sectarian club since 1892, and the long-serving Owen Brannigan for one was proud that their increased support, especially in the early '20s, was the result of their play rather than their origins, control of it had been just as tightly held as ever in the same few hands. The debenture holders nominated their own leaders, and Harry Swan and Wilson Terris joined the board. Swan's stay was neither uneventful nor unbroken, but by the middle of the decade he had the chairmanship. It was not universally popular either, because although never overtly anti-catholic, some of his measures and his alleged views certainly upset sections of Hibs' more traditional support.

Meanwhile, Hibs' results went from bad to worse. Yet another relegation battle loomed, this time with Ayr United, and although Hibs seemed to have seen off their rivals for the vital 18th spot with some games to go, after the final Saturday of the season the sides were level. Unfortunately Ayr had one game outstanding, they beat Kilmarnock by 1-0 and Hibs were consigned to the Second Division.

It was a bad time for Hibs – in their financial state, it was important to bounce right back, but they failed to do so. George Blyth had replaced Robb in goal, but he broke a leg against Edinburgh City and that did not help. Hibs finished seventh – or 27th in the Scottish League; they finished below teams like Forfar and Stenhousemuir, and, behind St. Bernards too with Leith Athletic in the First Division, were only the fourth-top Edinburgh team.

(Back row l to r) – Di Christopher, Buchanan, Duncan, Paterson, Harper, Shaw, Miller, Strong, T. Cannon and P. Cannon. (Seated) – Young, Halligan, Dunn, Director Owen Brannigan, Director John Farm, Director Alex Maley, Dornan, McGinnigle and Walker. The trophies – East of Scotland Shield, Dunedin Cup and Rosebery Bowl. The picture was taken in front of the old pavilion at Easter Road in May, 1922.

Willie Robb, noted for his taste in caps and long shorts, seen making one of many saves which earned Hibs a draw at Tynecastle in October 1928.

By the following year, however, things had improved; Hibs had regrouped, and some new faces were to be seen, notably Rab Walls and Peter Flucker up front. Hibs won fifteen out of their first eighteen games, and were never threatened in the promotion stakes. They had to win the title twice, because after they had first built up an unassailable lead, the league expelled two sides for not meeting guarantees, and six of Hibs' points were taken away. But the championship was never in doubt, and Hibs watched Queen of the South pip Dunfermline for second place behind them. There was also a new ground record of 33,759 for a cup-tie against Hearts, reflecting how much the fans were missing the derby games.

For the first two seasons back upstairs, Hibs consolidated successfully, surviving the first, and cruising along above halfway for most of the second before a string of defeats near the end. Ginger Watson earned a league cap for his rugged displays at centre-half, and Duncan Urquhart a full one. John Smith came from Hearts and then Jimmy Moffat from Motherwell to add class to the attack, and Peter Wilson, a clever and international wing-half, came from Celtic. With Tommy Egan coming through at left-half, Hibs now had a fine mid-line.

Things did not continue fine for long. In September 1936 Hibs went to Tynecastle and lost 8-3. It could have been worse because it was 6-0 shortly after half-time. Then came rumours that two Hibs men had been drinking before the game, and early the following week, Urquhart and Watson were freed – a risky move given Hibs' position. Another slide started, and in December, Hibs signed two Irishmen, "Soldier" Jones and Wm Gowdy, from Linfield. An Edinburgh

The Second Division champions of 1933. Back row (l to r) Langton, Watson, Wilkinson, Blyth, Urquhart and McFarlane. Front – Walls, Wallace, Halligan, Flucker and Hutchison.

bookmaker was believed to have sponsored the deal. It did not seem to help much – Hibs finished the year in second-bottom place by losing seven goals to Clyde.

Early in the new year, manager Templeton resigned, and was replaced by the unwilling caretaker, Johnny Halligan. Things continued in the same vein, and a home defeat from Ayr seemed critical. Hearts lent Hibs two players, goalkeeper Waugh and full back Munro, and when Hibs finally got a break, with just four games left, it was the young keeper who saved Hibs' bacon and two penalties at Rugby Park. A desperate last effort was made, and Hibs had to win at Dunfermline in the last game to survive.

It was arguably the most important game the club has played, and they won it by a single goal from Willie Black, the diminutive centre. It was a few days later that the importance of the win filtered through. Harry Swan had approached Willie McCartney, the flamboyant Hearts' manager until a year earlier, and McCartney had agreed to manage Hibs, but only if they stayed up. An appreciative crowd of 25,000 watched his first match in charge in the new season.

Hibs lost that one, and it seemed it would take some time to turn things round. Goalkeeper Gourlay and full back Prior were bought from Partick Thistle, and shorter-term signings included Johnny McKay, whose one cap had been earned thirteen years earlier. McCartney even tried to coax Barney Battles out of retirement, but the ex-Heart stayed put. By the end of December, Hibs were exactly where they were a year earlier – second bottom.

While this holding operation was being carried out, however, the long term was being catered for, and the finest band of youngsters for many a day was being brought together at Easter Road. There was Jimmy Kerr, a goalkeeper from Ormiston, Willie Finnegan from Bo'ness Cadora, who played even although he was supposed to be working on Saturday afternoons, Sammy Kean from Rob Roy and Tommy McIntyre from Portobello Renton. At the end of the season, a signing mix-up between Dundee United and Liverpool left Arthur Milne available briefly and McCartney swooped to sign him too.

It was a young and exciting team therefore which held a mid-table position for Hibs in the two years before the war. Their trademark was their volatility – some days they scored a lot of goals, and on other days they lost them. They lost three to Edinburgh City in January 1938, probably Hibs' most embarrassing cup reverse, but the following year they were unlucky to lose to Clyde in the semi-finals. It seemed appropriate too that, after a decade of grim survival, this renaissance should be associated with an altogether more cheerful strip, the bright green with "Arsenal"-style white sleeves replacing the plain dark green jerseys.

TALE OF A SPIDER AT EASTER ROAD

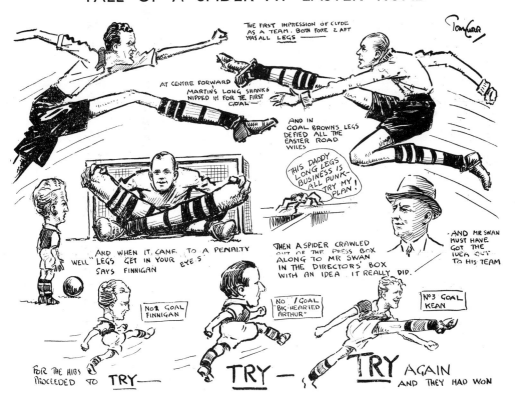

How Tom Curr saw the Hibs v Clyde in August 1939, two weeks before war caused the league programme to be abandoned.

CHAPTER 4

Wartime

"**G**IVE ME TEN YEARS AND I'LL MAKE HIBS GREAT" was Harry Swan's promise when he took control of the club. What he evidently did not foresee was Hitler's spanner in his works.

One feature of wartime football in Scotland was the unreality of chaotic travel and other arrangements, with players suddenly available or not, and allowed to guest for whomsoever their other commitments allowed. Another was the emergence of Hibs as the only serious challengers to Rangers. They were not unrelated. As with the 1914-18 war, the clubs furthest from the industrial west with its greater number of reserved occupations fared worst. Football north of the Forth was generally of reserve-team status and stopped altogether for a while, and even Hearts had an indifferent war. Hibs had Willie McCartney's silver tongue, and a steady stream of teenage talent and proven guests were persuaded to come to Easter Road.

The first season was a mixed one, however. The official programme was abandoned abruptly when war was declared, and it was late October before eastern and western divisions got under way. Hibs finished in mid-table, although they unearthed the country's top scorer in Johnny Cuthbertson, who was in the place of Arthur Milne, a guest of both Aberdeen and Dundee United. Another notable absentee was Tommy McIntyre, but Hibs had the services of Alex Hall, the Sunderland full back who stayed with Hibs throughout the war, Bob Kane (Leeds United), and the Adams-McLeod right-wing partnership from East Fife's 1938 cup-winning team.

By the following season, Bobby Baxter, Middlesbrough's Scottish international centre-half who had been guesting with Hearts, had moved across the city to skipper Hibs. The clubs had been unhappy with the financial strain of the regional leagues, and the top ones had formed the Southern League, with sixteen teams all from the Forth/Clyde valley. "Cubby" was again the League's top scorer, with 27 at more than one per game, before he too was whisked away to the war. He had three foursomes, against Falkirk, Queens Park and Clyde, but Rangers' rather unadventurous consistency won them the title, with Hibs in third place.

The summer of 1941 is not recalled by everyone as an especially happy time, but for Hibs' supporters it was magical. Firstly, at the end of April, manager McCartney blooded three seventeen-year-olds – Gordon Smith, Bobby Combe

"Li'l" Arthur Milne signed for Hibs from Dundee United in 1937, and was a crowd favourite till he left in 1946. The picture on the right was taken in 1987.

and Jock Weir – in the postponed derby against Hearts and saw them win 5-3. To add spice, the first two had been snatched from under the noses of the Tynecastle scouts. And this was followed up by the Liverpool and Scotland wing-half Matt Busby and the former St Johnstone and Everton winger Jimmy Caskie.

Success came on the pitch too. Largely the idea of Harry Swan, the Summer Cup competition was introduced. Arthur Milne returned to score a hat-trick at Parkhead in Hibs' progress to Hampden, to meet, inevitably, Rangers in the final. It seemed all over bar the shouting when Rangers went two up in the first quarter, but in a stirring turnaround, Willie Finnegan scored twice, one a penalty, and in the final minutes, Bobby Baxter made a rare excursion upfield to head a winner from a corner. The commentary of the latter stages was preserved on personalised gramophone records presented to the Hibs players, along with War

Willie McCartney, the charismatic Hibs manager who built Hibs for their post-war greatness, but who died just before their first league championship in 1948.

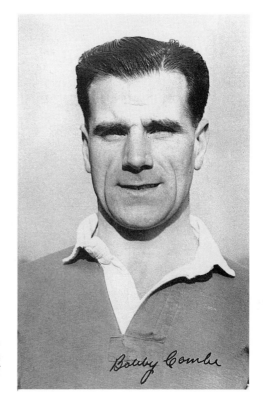

Bobby Combe, a prolific inside forward who became an international wing half. Among many achievements was the scoring of four goals in Hibs 8-1 thrashing of Rangers in 1941.

Savings Certificates. The team was Kerr; Shaw, Hall; Busby, Baxter, Kean; Nutley, Finnegan, Milne, Combe, Caskie.

So the gauntlet was thrown down. The rest of wartime football saw many oddities and comedies, but its important events were Hibs-Rangers classes. The 24 League points at stake between them were evenly shared, and Hibs' five victories were more than anyone else achieved against the Light Blues. If Rangers' greater strength in depth meant that they took every Southern League title, then only once were Hibs below third. Hibs and Rangers were also to contest a further three controversial cup finals.

The first of these was in the 1942 Summer Cup. Ibrox determination could scarcely have been greater, because since their defeat in the 1941 final, they had suffered an incredible 8-1 league defeat at Easter Road, and, to rub salt in the wound, Hibs had won the return at Ibrox too. The resulting Ibrox play was described as "rather ruthless", and Milne was reduced to passenger status within four minutes. But the remaining ten Hibs were equal to their opposition, and Davie Shaw struck the bar, the nearest either side came to scoring so that when Rangers took the trophy by toss of coin, their exuberant celebrations belied a somewhat hollow victory.

The 1944 League Cup final was curiously similar. When Jimmy Caskie won

The Hibs' party pictured at Hampden following their Summer Cup win of 1941. Back row (l to r) Gallacher, Anderson, Smith, Cummings, Gilmartin, Fleming and Cuthbertson. Middle – Mr. J. Drummond Shiels (Director), Adams, Shaw, Busby, Milne, Kean, Kerr, Hall and McColl (Assistant Trainer). Front – Nutley, Caskie, Mr. H. Swan (Chairman), Baxter, McCartney (Manager), Finnegan, Combe and Shaw (Trainer).

a last-minute corner, it was acclaimed as a goal by the Hibs' support, because it gave Hibs the trophy by six corners to five without a goal having been scored, and the Edinburgh fans showed a similarly scant degree of sympathy towards opponents who had lost their goalkeeper after just 17 minutes.

Whereas the war lasted six years, wartime football lasted seven, and finished in appropriate fashion with Hibs and Rangers contesting the Victory Cup final in the Spring of 1946. By this time Caskie had been transferred to Rangers and replaced by Queens Park's Johnny Aitkenhead; the new man scored a fine goal, but Rangers deserved their 3-1 win.

So where did the war leave Hibs? Clearly in a better state than most of their rivals, and poised for a real challenge for honours when peacetime competition resumed. Baxter had gone to Hearts again, but Peter Aird was established in his place and the other guests had gone home. Of the pre-war stars, Milne was now past thirty and Tommy McIntyre sadly never came home, but Kerr, Shaw, Kean, Finnigan and Nutley now provided a nucleus of experience. With Smith, Combe, Weir, Reilly, Govan, Howie and Archie Buchanan amongst the crop of wartime signings, August 1946 could not come soon enough.

Gordon Smith at centre against Queens Park in September 1941. Bobby Brown in goal is well beaten.

Three of Hibs' less publicised stars – from the left; John Grant, Jock Paterson and Tommy Preston.

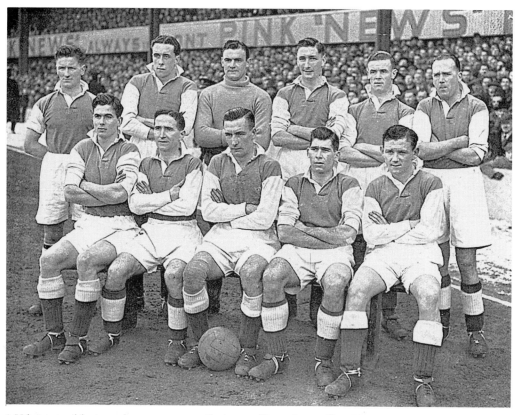

A Hibs' team of the immediate post-war era. Back row – Shaw, Govan, Kerr, Howie, Aird, Kean. Front – Smith, Finnegan, Cuthbertson, Turnbull, Ormond.

Two of Hibs' stars, Tommy Younger (left) and Bobby Johnstone, had a joint debut against Partick Thistle in March 1949.

CHAPTER 5

The Famous Five

HIBS' CHALLENGE TO RANGERS was posted early. Nine goals against Queen of the South in the first match was a warning, and four days later Hibs followed them up by winning by the odd goal in three at Ibrox before 60,000 spectators. When the return came round in December, there were long queues outside Easter Road when the gates opened at 11 a.m., three and a quarter hours before kick-off. When Rangers returned to Easter Road in a Scottish Cup replay in February, the all-ticket crowd of 50,000 was a ground record and when the Ibrox men took revenge for that 2-0 defeat by beating Hibs 3-1 in the League Cup semi-final at Hampden, there was a six-figure attendance. It was crowds like that which persuaded Harry Swan to draw up plans to extend the capacity of Easter Road to 98,000.

Even with three points out of four against Rangers, Hibs were unable to prevent the Light Blues from taking the league; Hibs were second, and they also reached the cup final, although only just. There was a ban on midweek football, so cup ties were played to a finish, and it took a fluke goal from defender Hugh Howie after 142 minutes to beat Motherwell in the semi-finals. In the final against Aberdeen, Johnny Cuthbertson scored within a minute, and Jimmy Kerr saved a penalty, but the Dons scored twice to lift the trophy.

Despite having had such a good season, however, Hibs were, like all other clubs after the war, trying to find the right blend. Their advantage was that Mr. McCartney had assembled a large squad of very good players, so that when Milne and Nutley were allowed to go, it still left players like Jock Brown, Govan, Buchanan, Cuthbertson, and the youngsters Reilly and Turnbull – in the reserves. First-team regulars included Kerr, Shaw, Howie, Kean, Smith, Finnegan, Combe, Weir and the red-haired Peter Aird, who had taken over from Bobby Baxter at centre-half.

Willie Ormond was signed from Stenhousemuir about the same time as Eddie Turnbull made the breakthrough into the big team. Jock Weir went to Blackburn for the first five-figure fee to cross the border, and that was reinvested in Leslie Johnstone, who came from Clyde for a Scottish record fee. Hibs were aiming high, and when Johnstone failed to fit in, they bought Alex Linwood, a wartime cap and a clinical finisher, from Middlesbrough. In the autumn of 1947, most of the Johnstone cash was reimbursed when the player returned to Shawfield.

Hibs in 1950: Back – Manager Shaw, Combe, Govan, Howie, Younger, Paterson, Cairns, Trainer McColl. Front – Smith, Johnstone, Reilly, Turnbull, Ormond.

Hibs' much vaunted new forward line – only Gordon Smith remained from a year before – did not start season 1947-48 just as well as they might, and in particular they suffered three defeats by Hearts in the first month or so. But soon the shoe was on the other foot, and when Hibs won the Ne'erday derby in style, they were top and the Tynecastle side was bottom. Hibs were playing well, and things were building up to what appeared to be a title decider with Rangers on the last day of January. The cup tie the week before, against Albion Rovers, did not seem to pose a problem.

Hibs won easily enough at Cliftonhill, but the whole event was overshadowed by the collapse and death of their manager, Willie McCartney, at the game. McCartney was such a larger-than-life character at the hub of Scottish football that his loss was felt as was only Jock Stein's in Cardiff in 1986. Hugh Shaw was immediately promoted from being Hibs' trainer, and his assistant Jimmy McColl became trainer.

The showdown with Rangers followed almost immediately. It produced an emotional finish, with Cuthbertson scoring the only goal in the last minute. Hibs

Brown, Young and Woodburn are all helpless to prevent Bobby Johnstone's late winner in a Scottish Cup tie at Ibrox in 1951.

seemed to go off the boil after that, and lost their advantage over Rangers, until Queens Park did them a favour by winning at Ibrox. Hibs scored five against Motherwell, which meant they could win the title at Dundee in their last game, but it wàs a big relief when Rangers slipped up again and they did not have to. Hibs were champions for the first time in forty-three years.

By now Hibs had something of a settled side, namely Kerr, Govan, Shaw, Kean, Howie, Buchanan, Smith, Combe, Linwood, Turnbull, and Ormond. Cuthbertson was next choice at inside forward, as Reilly was on either wing, notably when Ormond broke a leg in a cup tie against Aberdeen. George Farm was Kerr's deputy after he was hurt in the same game, and played his only nine first-team games before going to Blackpool. This run included the semi-final of the cup at Hampden when Rangers won 1-0 in front of more than 143,000

John Paterson clears off the line with Willie Ormond ready to help, in the Coronation Cup Final at Hampden in 1953.

spectators. Hibs' achievement in winning the league was recognised when five of them, Govan, Smith, Combe, Shaw and Turnbull, were selected together for Scotland against Belgium.

Hibs' defence of their first post-war title was less impressive. They dropped too many points early on, especially at home, and were top of the league at the end of November only because Rangers and Dundee had games in hand. One feature of this period was the play of Lawrie Reilly on the left wing, but even so, it was a surprise when he was chosen to play in Cardiff for Scotland in that position. There were only three horses in the race for the league, but Hibs finished third.

Meanwhile Linwood had been transferred to Clyde, and Plumb and Cuthbertson each failed to impress at centre. Then Willie Ormond came back,

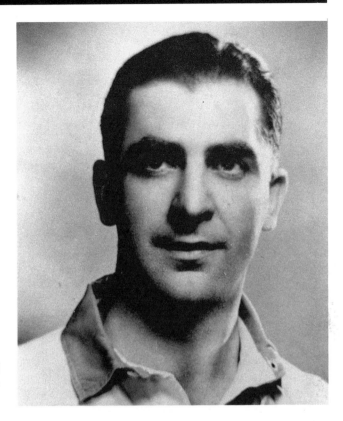

Alex Linwood, a wartime cap and clinical finisher, signed for Hibs from Middlesbro' in 1947.

Reilly switched into the middle, and the centre-forward problem was solved for the next decade or so. In the spring, with the league conceded, manager Shaw introduced Tommy Younger in goal, John Paterson, an Englishman, at centre-half, where there had been something of a problem since Hugh Howie's health had failed, and Bobby Johnstone, who had been earning rave notices in the reserves.

There was a lot of competition for places, but it was only the performance in the 1949 league cup semi-final against Dunfermline which persuaded manager Shaw to make decisive changes. Hibs had reached that stage rather unconvincingly, including losing four goals at Firhill in the first leg of the quarter finals, and when they lost 2-1 at Tynecastle to second division opponents after scoring first, action was demanded. The entire half-back line of Gallagher, McNeil and Cairns was scrapped, and a new one of Combe, Paterson and Buchanan brought in instead; defensively it was a risky strategy because both Combe and Buchanan had been forwards.

Much attention was given to this new-look half-back line, and it played a big part in Hibs' successes of the next few years, but it seemed almost incidental that Combe's move back opened the door for Johnstone, and that a week after

Tommy Younger in spectacular form during the 1953 Coronation Cup Final against Celtic.

the defeat by Dunfermline, the Hibs' attack read Smith, Johnstone, Reilly, Turnbull, Ormond for the first time in a competitive match.

It was not long before people took notice. By the end of December Hibs had taken twenty-three points out of twenty-four, only a last-minute equaliser at Parkhead preventing a clean sweep. Meanwhile, Hearts had notched up ten straight wins, and so the derby on January 2nd was a matter of the keenest anticipation. Edinburgh football's biggest crowd, 65,850, crammed into Easter Road to see the Tynecastle side come from behind to beat Hibs 2-1.

Hibs lost only one more league game, when Lew Goram, father of Andy, played his only first-team game at Easter Road – on loan from Hibs to Third Lanark, and kept a clean sheet. They still failed to pull away from Rangers, however, and needed to win their last game, at Ibrox, to clinch the title. The score was 0-0. Rangers then needed a draw in their last game, against Third Lanark, and they got it when Thirds missed a late penalty with the score 2-2.

There was great excitement at Easter Road, and a feeling that Hibs were now equipped to take over. Already the interchanging of positions for which the five forwards were to become renowned was in evidence, with Smith to the fore

Another championship celebration, this time in 1952. Back – trainer McColl, Combe, Howie, Paterson, Younger, manager Shaw, Govan, Gallagher, Buchanan, assistant trainer Kean. Front – Mr. Terris (director), Johnstone, Smith, Mr. Swan (chairman), Reilly, Turnbull, Ormond, Mr. Hartland (director).

with his willingness to cut through the centre, and defenders unsure how to alter their traditional game to cope. Hibs won the 1950-51 championship by ten points, and with four games to spare. The title was clinched with four second-half goals at Shawfield, when only Turnbull of the regular front line was playing, and the season finished with Rangers and Celtic being trounced in the same weekend.

It was only the daunting combination of Motherwell and Lady Luck which prevented a clean sweep of the honours. Hibs had survived a 4-1 deficit in the first leg of their league cup quarter-final at Pittodrie, and a semi-final visit to their cup bogey ground at Tynecastle, and seemed certain to win the final against Motherwell, against whom they had scored six league goals a week earlier. For over an hour, it seemed Hibs must win, then suddenly Motherwell struck twice, and Hibs lost 3-0.

The Scottish Cup semi was even more of a disaster, against the same opponents at Tynecastle. Motherwell were gifted a lucky goal in the first minute, full back John Ogilvie broke a leg, and Willie Ormond ruptured ligaments, and nine Hibs did well just to lose 3-2.

Hibs win this league match against Motherwell by 3-1, played in January 1951. Gordon Smith beats Hamilton to the ball.

Hibs' defence of their title was again less convincing than their winning of it. Every now and again they seemed to have recaptured their form, and certainly they kept on winning, but not with the same aplomb. Apart from the result, the league campaign was an unsatisfactory affair – Hibs were miles ahead by early 1952, largely because their first stage exit from both cups had enabled them to play more games than Rangers, and it was a question of whether Rangers could take enough points from the games in hand. Just once, when Hibs lost 5-2 at Dumfries was it a serious possibility. Meanwhile, Hibs had just one home Saturday game after March 1st, and played out the season with a series of friendlies, mainly in England; home fans only got an extra ration of St. Mirren and a visit from Bolton Wanderers.

An Eddie Turnbull special from the penalty spot against Rapid Vienna in 1951.

Goals Galore

"THE GOOD MEN DO LIVES AFTER THEM, the bad is oft interred with their bones", to paraphrase Mark Antony. Those who watched Hibs in the early 'fifties recount tales of high scores week after week, with little thought of defence. In fact, the Famous Five never reached a hundred league goals in a season, and their highest total was 93 in 1952-53. By that time the Hibs' support had donned a mantle of arrogance more usually associated with teams from Glasgow and often with less cause.

There was a certain arrogance on the pitch too, with the belief that, even if goals were conceded, the forwards would pull them back. Rangers played a more traditional game, and when the final whistle blew on the season, and the two sides had the same number of points, the Rangers' goal average was the better.

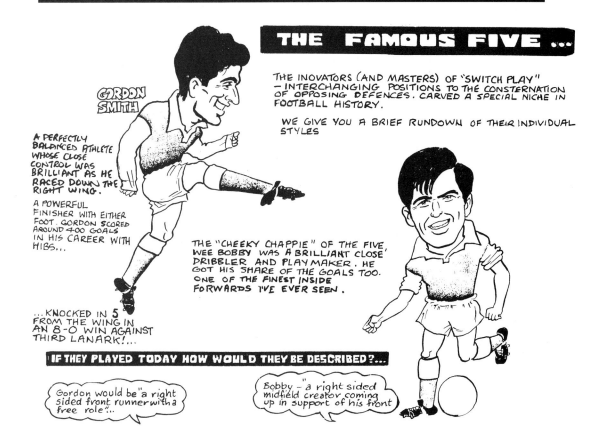

THE FAMOUS FIVE ...

GORDON SMITH

THE INOVATORS (AND MASTERS) OF "SWITCH PLAY" — INTERCHANGING POSITIONS TO THE CONSTERNATION OF OPPOSING DEFENCES. CARVED A SPECIAL NICHE IN FOOTBALL HISTORY.

WE GIVE YOU A BRIEF RUNDOWN OF THEIR INDIVIDUAL STYLES

A PERFECTLY BALANCED ATHLETE WHOSE CLOSE CONTROL WAS BRILLIANT AS HE RACED DOWN THE RIGHT WING.

A POWERFUL FINISHER WITH EITHER FOOT. GORDON SCORED AROUND 400 GOALS IN HIS CAREER WITH HIBS...

THE "CHEEKY CHAPPIE" OF THE FIVE, WEE BOBBY WAS A BRILLIANT CLOSE DRIBBLER AND PLAYMAKER. HE GOT HIS SHARE OF THE GOALS TOO. ONE OF THE FINEST INSIDE FORWARDS I'VE EVER SEEN.

...KNOCKED IN 5 FROM THE WING IN AN 8-0 WIN AGAINST THIRD LANARK!...

IF THEY PLAYED TODAY HOW WOULD THEY BE DESCRIBED?...

Gordon would be "a right sided front runner with a free role"...

Bobby – a right sided midfield creator coming up in support of his front

Had it been goal difference, it would have been the other way round, but goal difference was several years away. But both sides dropped more points than in recent seasons, which may have been the first indications that these two great post-war sides had peaked.

In all games that season, Hibs scored five or more on fifteen occasions, including seven against Motherwell home and away, and another seven against Manchester United, the English champions. Reilly was the country's top scorer with thirty league goals. As always, cups proved elusive – Dundee were the latest to benefit from Hibs' Tynecastle hoodoo in the league cup, Aberdeen won a quarter-final replay in the Scottish, and Hibs outplayed Celtic in the Coronation Cup final only to lose 2-0 to them.

The Coronation Cup seemed to be a watershed. By the start of the next season, Reilly was wanting a transfer, and in dispute because he was not awarded a benefit. He was not long back when he became ill in early 1954, and missed most of the year, and the World Cup. Early in 1955, Johnstone was transferred to England. Smith had broken a leg in 1954 and Buchanan had knee problems, while Govan and Howie had been replaced by Willie McFarlane and Pat Ward.

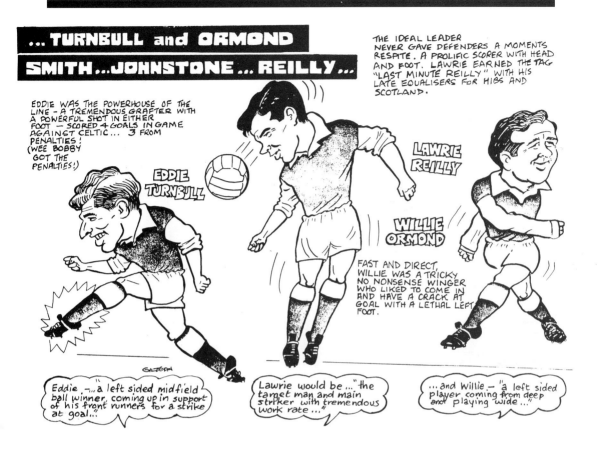

... TURNBULL and ORMOND SMITH ... JOHNSTONE ... REILLY ...

THE IDEAL LEADER NEVER GAVE DEFENDERS A MOMENTS RESPITE. A PROLIFIC SCORER WITH HEAD AND FOOT. LAWRIE EARNED THE TAG "LAST MINUTE REILLY" WITH HIS LATE EQUALISERS FOR HIBS AND SCOTLAND.

EDDIE WAS THE POWERHOUSE OF THE LINE - A TREMENDOUS GRAFTER WITH A POWERFUL SHOT IN EITHER FOOT — SCORED 4 GOALS IN GAME AGAINST CELTIC ... 3 FROM PENALTIES! (WEE BOBBY GOT THE PENALTIES!)

EDDIE TURNBULL

LAWRIE REILLY

WILLIE ORMOND

FAST AND DIRECT, WILLIE WAS A TRICKY NO NONSENSE WINGER WHO LIKED TO COME IN AND HAVE A CRACK AT GOAL WITH A LETHAL LEFT FOOT.

Eddie – "a left sided midfield ball winner, coming up in support of his front runners for a strike at goal ..."

Lawrie would be ..." the target man and main striker with tremendous work rate ..."

... and Willie – "a left sided player coming from deep and playing wide ..."

By the end of 1954, Jimmy Thomson, Tommy Preston and Jackie Plenderleith were figuring in first team line-ups, so that less than half of the team had championship medals.

Appreciation

THE LEAST CONTROVERSIAL ACCOUNT of Hibs' greatest side is a statistical one. Briefly, Hibs may have won three post-war championships to Rangers' four, but they were within an ace of taking five out of seven, and four in a row. They took more points than the Ibrox team in these seven seasons, and scored 113 more league goals. In direct matches between the sides, Hibs won 6 league games and lost three, with the Ibrox men ahead 3-2 in cup ties. In cup ties, however, Hibs had an amazing jinx at Tynecastle – they played semi-finals there against Queen of the South, Dunfermline, East Fife, Motherwell and Dundee, and beat only the Dumfriesians.

From the fifties, Jackie Plenderleith, left, later capped by Scotland, and Willie McFarlane, who returned to Hibs as manager.

All five forwards scored a hundred league goals for Hibs by the end of their careers, and Lawrie Reilly was Scotland's top scorer three times in a row, as well as being the country's most capped forward. Gordon Smith had his own fan club, and remains Scottish football's highest-scoring winger, lying fifth in the all-time scoring lists. Each of the Famous Five won at least as many full caps as the Hearts' inside forward trio of the late 'fifties to whom they are sometimes compared, and behind them, Younger, Govan, Howie, Shaw, and Combe all won full caps, and even the English-born Paterson played for the Scottish League.

How can one summarise Hibs' championship winning side? Firstly, of course, Manager Shaw inherited a lot of very good players, and a first-class youth policy was the reason for that. Only Willie Ormond came from another senior side, and he cost a very modest fee. Hibs retained a lot of youngsters, and their second and third strings were well nigh unbeatable in their respective spheres of operation.

If Willie McCartney takes the greatest part of the credit for the playing personnel, chairman Harry Swan was responsible for taking Hibs into Europe, at a time when foreigners were thought of as people who played across the park and couldn't shoot. Football in the fifties was not the tactical exercise it is today, but Hibs learned from their frequent trips abroad; their heyday coincided with that

Hibs parading the League Championship trophy in 1951. Back – Paterson, trainer McColl, Buchanan, Younger, manager Shaw, Govan, Ogilvie, Sounness, assistant trainer Kean, Gallagher. Seated – Mr. Terris (director), Reilly, Combe, Mr. Swan (chairman), Smith, Ormond, Mr. Hartland (director). Front – Johnstone and Turnbull.

of the famous Hungarian international side, and Hibs' style took more from the Magyars' way of playing than any other British side.

Another aspect of Swan's vision for football was the use of floodlights. Hibs were impressed by the lights of the Racing Club of Paris in 1951, and they also took part in the first UK experiment at Stenhousemuir the same year. When they hanselled their own lights in the autumn of 1954, they were the best there were, and the first major lighting system in Scotland. As an indication of the attitudes of other clubs at the time, Aberdeen refused to play under the Easter Road lights as late as 1957. Hibs' prominence in both of these fields made them an ideal club to represent Scotland in the first European Cup.

Eddie Turnbull's drive flashes past Ronnie Simpson to open the scoring in the Coronation Cup match between Hibs and Newcastle United at Ibrox. Hibs won 4-0.

The European Cup

THE EUROPEAN CUP WAS LAUNCHED IN 1955-56 by a French newspaper, and Hibs were invited to represent Scotland. Invitations were not issued to national champions but to the teams whose appeal would most likely make the tournament a success. Hibs had been the most pro-European club in Britain, and had toured extensively, from Czechoslovakia in 1946, and even including a visit to Brazil in 1953. It was just a little unfortunate that l'Equipe had not got their tournament off the ground five years earlier.

Hibs' achievement, especially in the first round, tends to be played down, and at the time, not one national newspaper sent a representative. West Germany were holders of the World Cup, and Rotweiss Essen were their champions, with a formidable reputation against foreign opposition, including a highly successful tour of South America. Hibs' performance in beating them 4-0 in the Rhineland mud was magnificent, and the return-leg score of 1-1 has to be taken in the context of Younger, Smith and Reilly being replaced by last-minute substitutes after that trio had been delayed on the return-leg of an international trip.

The next opponents were Djurgaarden of Stockholm, and because of the Scandinavian winter, both games were played in Scotland – the Swedes electing to play their "home" game under Partick Thistle's new lights at Firhill. Hibs won 3-1 in Glasgow, and 1-0 in a poor game in Edinburgh.

That put them into the semi-finals, where despite valiant efforts, they lost

Tommy Younger saves from Sandberg, the outside left of Djurgaarden, in the European Cup match played at Firhill in November 1955. John Paterson (no. 3) looks on.

Rheims goalkeeper Jacquet punches clear during the European Cup semi-final against Hibs in Paris. Willie Ormond is prevented by Zimmy from doing very much about it.

Gordon Smith with Tommy Walker. Both players scored hat-tricks in Smith's debut for Hibs at Tynecastle in April 1941. Hibs won 5-3.

to Reims of France. A last-minute goal in France gave the Frenchmen a two-goal cushion they did not merit, but it mattered little, because Hibs were unable to break through even once at Easter Road, and Reims broke away to score late on and kill the tie. The crowd of 45,000 was a floodlit record.

End Of An Era

ALL GOOD THINGS COME TO AN END, and the Famous Five were no exception. The first problem was Lawrie Reilly's illness. The centre recovered, and was back in the international side when the famous Hungarian side visited Hampden in November 1954, and he was capped as late as the Wembley match of 1957, but the illness had taken its toll.

By the start of 1955, Hibs were playing second fiddle to the rising Hearts team; in January of that year they twice conceded five goals at Tynecastle, and in addition, Bobby Johnstone was transferred to Manchester City for £22,000.

Gordon Smith was thirty-four, but was selected as Scotland's captain for the 1955 tour of Austria and Hungary. A year later, goalkeeper Tommy Younger went to Liverpool, and Hibs were forced to field a most inexperienced defence, which was therefore less equipped than its predecessor to provide the service for its attack. When Bobby Combe was reintroduced to the forward line, shortly before he retired, the front five totalled sixty years' service, but there was no turning back the clock.

By now, Hibs were no more than a middle of the table team, and despite having a successful reserve side, the players coming through too often failed to make the grade. When Hibs reached the 1958 cup final, Reilly had just returned, Smith was recovering from having bone fragments removed from an ankle, and Turnbull, now also a veteran, was lending his experience from right-half, a position from which he captained Scotland's World Cup campaign in Sweden. One felt that the final against Clyde was the last chance for Turnbull and Ormond, both survivors of the 1947 cup final side, and that it was indeed the end of an era.

It was, although for Gordon Smith in particular there was a considerable Indian Summer; dismissed by Hibs in 1959 on a free transfer, Smith had the operation he needed privately, and went on to win league championship medals with both Hearts and Dundee, and represent both in the European Cup.

Eddie Turnbull retired in 1959 and joined the backroom staff, and Willie Ormond played until 1961 before ending his career with Falkirk.

Hibs in transition in 1958. Back row – Trainer W. Hunter, MacLeod, Grant, McLelland, Leslie, Paterson, Turnbull, Plenderleith, Baxter. Front – Fraser, Aitken, Baker, Reilly, Preston, Ormond.

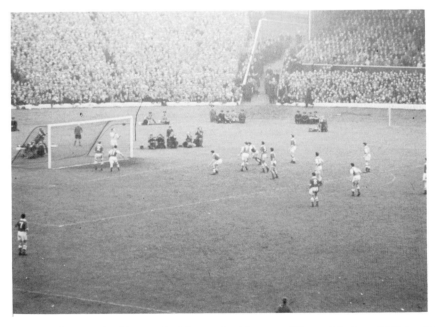

This picture shows the considerable appeal of the cup final between Hibs and Clyde in 1958. Joe Baker has a powerful header well held, with Willie Ormond in close attendance.

CHAPTER 6

The Sixties

THE LEGACY of the successful side of the early 'fifties at the end of the decade was that Hibs had a nucleus of veteran players from the former era, and a crop of younger players; what they lacked was something in between, players in the middle of their careers able to take over from the more senior men as they finished their careers. Of the younger brigade, John Grant and Johnny Macleod were capped while still with Hibs, Jackie Plenderleith and Lawrie Leslie after leaving, and Nicol, Harrower and Baxter won under-23 honours, so that there was a fair sprinkling of talent, but the outstanding prospect at the time was undoubtedly Joe Baker.

Baker was of English birth, and came into the Hibs team as Reilly's deputy during 1957-58, the latter's last season. His first goal was against Hearts when Hibs won 4-2 in hanselling the Tynecastle floodlights, and in February 1958, he scored four goals against the same opponents to win an incredible cup tie 4-3. In the year when Hearts were regarded as invincible, it is not always remembered that a very young Hibs' team twice beat them at Tynecastle.

In the autumn of 1958, the return of Gordon Smith gave us just a glimpse of what might have been the result of allying the skills of the Famous Five to the aggression and speed of Baker, which none of his contemporaries could match – Baker scored eighteen goals in nine games. With Smith and Turnbull going in 1959, Hibs felt it necessary to buy some experience, and brought Bobby Johnstone back from Manchester City. By now, Baker had been joined in the first team by the equally pacy Johnny Macleod, and a goal avalanche followed.

In a single week, Hibs scored twenty-three goals, seven against Dunfermline, five against Bolton, and eleven at Broomfield, a British "away" record. Eight weeks later, they scored ten against Partick Thistle at Firhill, and when Walter Winterbottom, English team manager, came up to see Baker and his rival for the centre-forward place at under-23 level, Brian Clough, he saw an amazing 6-6 draw between Hibs and Middlesbrough. Baker was capped for England at under-23 level, and at full international level, while still a teenager.

While Hibs were in a mid-table position and scoring goals, there was little panic about a defence which conceded nearly as many. In 1959-60, Hibs scored 106 league goals, Baker claiming 42, but they conceded 85. In 1959, they lost all six league cup section games, and in 1961 they lost their opening eight league

Joe Baker, capped for England as a teenager, and Hibs' most prolific goalscorer of all.

games. These were not the statistics of a top team, and it seemed all was not right behind the scenes either. It seemed incredible that Harry Swan, a man of such vision a decade before, should fail to see the short-term implications of selling Joe Baker, who had not asked for a transfer, instead of granting the modest salary increase that would have kept him at Easter Road; Johnny Macleod also went, to Arsenal.

It seemed that Swan's long reign must end soon, and the same was expected of Hugh Shaw, near retiral age. It was in October 1961 that chairman and manager parted over a disagreement, Shaw going briefly to Raith Rovers. Swan replaced him with Walter Galbraith, the virtually unknown manager of Tranmere Rovers.

Walter Galbraith

WALTER GALBRAITH is not regarded as having been Hibs' most successful or popular boss, and there were certainly those who did not take to the Clark Gable image that he projected, but the truth was that what he took over at Easter Road was a manager's nightmare. The team had been held in a mid-table position largely by the goalscoring of the two young forwards who had been transferred, and of the experienced men, Ormond left Hibs in 1961, and Sammy Baird, bought to replace Bobby Johnstone and so influential particularly against the continentals, was nearing the close of his career. Moreover, Galbraith and trainer Turnbull did not see eye to eye, and the latter, feeling spurned about the former's appointment in any case, went to train Queens Park.

Even with Gerry Baker replacing his brother and Ally Macleod his kinsman, Galbraith was left with a pool which would have difficulty holding its own in the First Division. Just how badly off they were became clearer in 1962-63.

The season was remarkable for the severity of the weather, and when Hibs took the field against Third Lanark on March 9th, they had fully half their league campaign to go. This was important because they had amassed only ten points, and seemed to be stranded with Raith in the relegation positions. Hibs lost league doubles to Airdrie, Clyde and Falkirk, and at one time were nine points behind the Shawfield side who were third bottom. It was against Airdrie that the well known incident took place when a young fan took the ball up to the highest point of the terracing and kicked it away. A catalogue of injuries meant that Hibs were allowed to sign Willie Toner to be their ninth centre half, well after the transfer deadline.

A first-half hat-trick by Baker at Dundee, a last-minute own goal at Firhill, and three goals in five minutes during an amazing lapse by Hearts' defenders at Tynecastle kept a flicker of hope alive, but with three games to go, Hibs were

Johnny Graham and Peter Marinello pictured in a Scottish Cup match at Firs Park, Falkirk in 1967–68.

still four points behind Clyde with an inferior goal average. But Hibs beat St. Mirren and Queen of the South while Clyde lost to Celtic, so that when Hibs won 4-0 at Kirkcaldy on May 20th, it left Clyde to score eight against Rangers to stay up.

At last, action was taken. It was in 1963 that Harry Swan decided to quit, handing over to William P. Harrower, a local bookmaker; for a man who had been so instrumental in bringing about Hibs' greatest days, it was ironic that his chairmanship should end with the team as far down as the league as when it began in the 'thirties. Money was now made available, and Galbraith brought Willie Hamilton, Neil Martin, Pat Quinn and John Parke to the club. He should also be remembered as the man who brought in youngsters like Cormack, O'Rourke and Stanton to the side, and suddenly Hibs were unrecognisable from the struggling outfit of a year earlier. A number of injuries meant that it was the spring of 1964 before this was translated into results and a move up the table, at which point Galbraith resigned and returned to England.

Neil Martin, deadly in front of goal, and scorer of over forty goals in one season.

The great Willie Hamilton with Pat Quinn.

Jock Stein

HIBS HAD TRIED TO GET JOCK STEIN, the up-and-coming Dunfermline manager, in 1961 and had been rebuffed, but in 1964 they were successful. If Galbraith had vindicated his reputation as a manager who knew good players, then Stein it was who quickly moulded them into a fine team. The new manager had to add only John MacNamee, the giant Celtic centre-half, to his pool.

Success was almost instant. Hibs qualified for the later stages of the Summer Cup, although they needed Hearts to go to America and a play-off with Dunfermline to make it. They swept past Kilmarnock and beat Aberdeen 3-1 at Pittodrie in a replayed final held over until the new season because of a typhoid epidemic in Aberdeen.

Stein was the first of the new tracksuit style of manager at Easter Road, and brought a new authority and discipline to the club. No-one benefitted more than Willie Hamilton, whose unparalleled skills were now seen to the full. Stein also solved the problem of playing two such similar players as Hamilton and Quinn, by moving the latter to just in front of the defence, a tactic which worked to perfection when Stein engineered Real Madrid's famous defeat at Easter Road in October 1964, and their even more impressive rout of Rangers at Ibrox a few days later.

By early 1965, Hibs were genuine championship contenders with Hearts, Kilmarnock and Dunfermline, and the completed their first league double over

Jock Stein, Tommy Younger, Tom Hart at Hibs' centenary celebrations.

Rangers since 1902-03. They also put the Ibrox side out of the cup with a Willie Hamilton double, but the euphoria of that win was shattered by the announcement that Stein was leaving to manage Celtic after only less than a year in Edinburgh. Not surprisingly Hibs faltered just enough to lose contact with the leaders, and Kilmarnock and Hearts were left to enact the season's final drama.

Bob Shankly

EDDIE TURNBULL AND JOHN PRENTICE were reckoned to be the front runners for the manager's job, and so Bob Shankly, brother of Liverpool's Bill, was a surprise choice. Shankly certainly had the credentials for the job – he was manager of Dundee, and had taken them to the 1962 championship, and the semi-finals of the European Cup, in some style.

Since then, however, he had become disillusioned over his inability to prevent the break-up of that side, and a feature of his stay at Easter Road was the

Bob Shankly joined Hibs as manager more than fifteen years after Sammy Kean retired as a player. Here they are pictured in New York while on tour with Dundee.

Peter Cormack as ever in the thick of the action – in this case against St. Johnstone.

constant transfer talk, and Shankly's determination to hold onto his star players. Most of the talk seemed to concern Peter Cormack, so it was a little ironic that Cormack should still be with Hibs when Shankly eventually resigned over Colin Stein's transfer to Rangers.

Although there was a steady drift south of players, Hibs had a more settled look than for some time. Willie Wilson regained his in-goal place from Ronnie Simpson, who went to Celtic, and his full backs were Bobby Duncan and Joe Davis, signed from Third Lanark to replace the departed John Parke. Both were fast ball-playing backs rather than just tacklers. Centre-half was John MacNamee, and when the twin centre-half system came in, he was joined by Pat Stanton to make a formidable barrier. Ultimately McNamee had to go to Newcastle to avoid refereeing disfavour, and he was replaced by Morton's stocky Dane, John Madsen. John Baxter completed the rear half of the team.

Up front there were the considerable skills of Jim Scott, Peter Cormack,

The Ne'erday derby of 1970 – Peter Cormack in trouble with referee Gordon while Stanton, Graham, McBride and Schaedler help plead his case.

Willie Hamilton, Pat Quinn and Eric Stevenson together with the graft of Jimmy O'Rourke and the goalscoring panache of Neil Martin. If this team had a fault, it was the lack of muscle up front and in midfield – allowed to play football, as they were against Jock Stein's Celtic, they contributed to the most thrilling of matches, whereas they all too often found problems against sides like Rangers with lesser skills, but a more "committed" attitude. There was little to doubt that Hibs had better footballers than any other side in the league except Celtic, but they only once made the top three.

Apart from McNamee, three big names went south; Neil Martin wanted away to further his career in English football, and was transferred to Sunderland, while Willie Hamilton's lifestyle and attitude were no longer held to be fully compensated by his ball skills, and he was transferred to Aston Villa. Later on, Jim Scott also went to Newcastle. New signings over the same period included Jim Scott's elder brother Alex from Everton, Alan Cousin, an elegant half-back who had been under Shankly at Dundee, and Allan McGraw, who had been a prolific goalscorer with Morton, but slotted into a midfield role at Easter Road.

One who did not go south was Colin Stein, a strong bustling centre-forward signed from Armadale, who had become quite a favourite with Hibs' fans. Shankly resisted to the full when Stein went away, but ultimately bowed to the inevitable, and Hibs negotiated terms with Everton, only for Stein to turn them down. Then Rangers made a similar bid, and Stein became the first six-figure transfer between Scottish clubs. His replacement was the veteran Celt, Joe McBride who scored a lot of goals during his time at Easter Road, but Bob Shankly resigned in disgust. He was persuaded to return, but without the same enthusiasm, and left early in 1969-70.

Willie McFarlane

THIS TIME IT WAS WILLIE McFARLANE, former Hibs' fullback and a likeable extrovert, who was the successful applicant; he was the part-time boss of Stirling Albion, but reverted to full-time at Easter Road. McFarlane's tenure was a short one – little over a year – but a colourful one.

He first persuaded the transfer-bent Cormack to sign another contract, and had also to deal with the precocious teenage winger, Peter Marinello, who was making English scouts take notice. McFarlane found it just as hard to keep players as his predecessor, and Marinello went to Arsenal at New Year. Meanwhile, Cormack's frustration at his friend getting away resulted in misbehaviour on the pitch and the concomitant suspensions, and he was transferred to Nottingham Forest later in the season. With a third of the Marinello cash, McFarlane bought Arthur Duncan from Partick Thistle, and who is to say that was a bad bit of business? He also bought centre-half Jim Black from Airdrie – Madsen had gone back to Denmark – and brought Erich Schaedler from Stirling.

It was in the autumn of 1970 that Bill Harrower gave over to Tom Hart, an East Lothian builder who was to do much for Hibs. Hart was an autocratic chairman, and he soon learned the hard way where his authority stopped, when, before the end of the year, he lost his manager over the latter's refusal to compromise his rights in team selection.

A sparse crowd on the old terracing share Arthur Duncan's excitement over the goalkeeping antics in front of him.

CHAPTER 7

The Seventies

S O HIBS STARTED OFF 1971 with another new manager. This time it was Dave Ewing, who had earned a considerable reputation as a coach in England before coming to Hibs in that capacity. Now in charge, he introduced the cautious English style of player to Easter Road, and looked for different qualities in his players. Marshall, Shevlane, Schaedler, McBride, Graham and Jim Blair, an expensive signing from St. Mirren, were all discarded, and only Schaedler ever regained his place. But the new style was not attractive, popular or successful, and Hibs finished twelfth. Ewing resigned after these few months to take a coaching position down south; he is primarily remembered for a carelessly expressed view to the press that "Rangers are rubbish".

No-one could accuse Hibs this time of not thinking big. Eddie Turnbull was the man who had transformed Aberdeen in the latter 'sixties and taken them to two cup finals, but he left the Dons because Hibs were the club who mattered most to him. He inherited a talented but disorganised bunch of players, possibly the most gifted team ever to finish as low as twelfth, and initially added just two players – former Dunfermline goalkeepr Jim Herriot, at the time in South Africa, and the Fifers' playmaker Alex Edwards. Centre-forward remained a problem for a time – Joe Baker had come home to an emotional welcome in February 1971, but had an injured hip which was failing to heal. In January 1972, Turnbull decided that he had waited long enough, and bought Alan Gordon from Dundee United.

By the spring of 1972, it was noticeable that many weaknesses had been addressed. Arthur Duncan's phenomenal speed was now allied to greater accuracy in crossing when he hit the bye-line, while on the right, Johnny Hamilton was more involved than of yore. Jim Black was winning the ball in the air, and Alan Gordon, always thought of as a casual type of player, now harried and hustled. At the back, Brownlie's natural flair was allied to timing in the tackle, and Schaedler had improved out of all recognition. Hibs finished third in the league, and made the cup final. Turnbull had obviously learnt more at coaching school than charm school, but Wilson Humphries came as coach, and was something of a smoothing influence, so that for the time being, everything went well.

Turnbull had said that it would take three years for his team to develop, and

Joe Baker, in his second spell with Hibs, lets fly at the Motherwell goal. Kenny Davidson is well up with play.

the cup final came to early for them – Hibs were not equipped to take on Jock Stein's Celtic who had reached the European Cup final the previous year, and in the end they were crushed 6-1, but in getting there they demonstrated that they and not Rangers were the only credible opposition to the Parkhead men with as one-sided a semi-final win as had been seen against the Ibrox team for many a year.

A quick rematch with both halves of the Old Firm came with the 1972 Drybrough Cup. In the semi-final, Hibs shrugged aside the intended intimidation of Greig, Macdonald and co., and trounced Rangers, the 3-0 scoreline doing them scant justice. They met Celtic again at Hampden, and won by 5-3 after extra time. These successes said much for the character of the team – Rangers supporters, fresh from Barcelona, brought the semi-final to a halt when Hibs opened the scoring, and Celtic fans did likewise in the final when Hibs were coasting along three goals in front. The interruption upset their play. Celtic scored three times before close, and it was a terrific performance for Hibs to come back with goals from substitute Jimmy O'Rourke and Arthur Duncan in the extra half-hour.

From a comparatively subdued league cup section in which Hibs and Aberdeen went through easily from Queens Park and Queen of the South,

Six Celtic defenders surround him, but Joe Harper still manages to score for Hibs in the 1974 League Cup final.

momentum built up through the autumn; goals started to flow and there was no more exciting team in the country than Hibs. In the league cup knock-out stages, Hibs twice trailed at Airdrie, before hammering their hosts 6-2, while they were two down at Tannadice and won 5-2. In the European Cupwinners' Cup, they scored five second-half goals to beat Sporting Lisbon 6-1, their biggest European defeat, and went one better against Besa of Albania in their next tie.

European football took its winter break, but the league cup carried on. John Brownlie scored the only goal as Hibs beat Rangers in another semi-final, so that Hibs qualified to meet, inevitably, Celtic in another final. Jock Stein paid Hibs

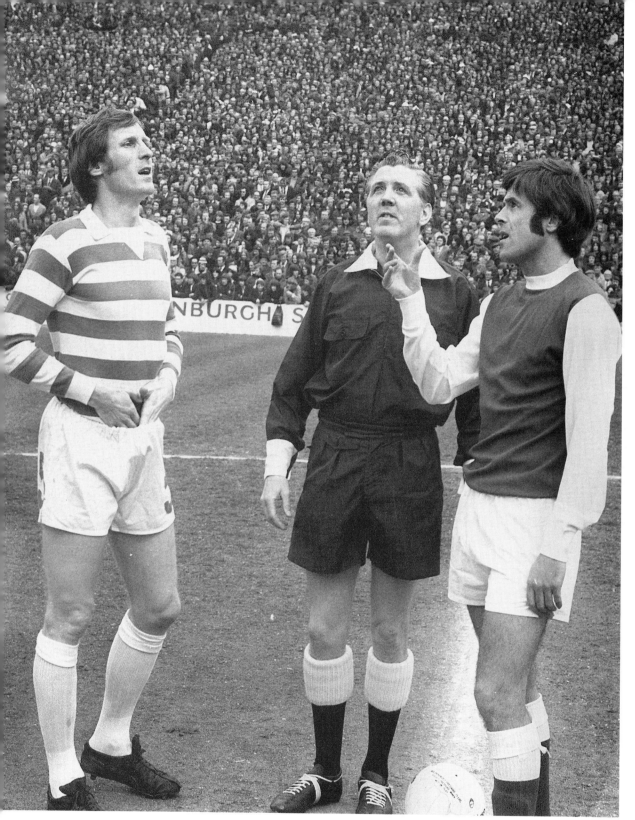

Pat Stanton and Billy McNeill toss up before another Hibs–Celtic clash at Easter Road.

Pat Stanton holds the Drybrough Cup aloft, and Jim McArthur salutes the crowd after the 1973 final.

the compliment of playing Jimmy Johnstone on the left to curb Brownlie, but it made little difference; Hibs had such a head of steam at this time that they might have had more than the second-half goals by Stanton and O'Rourke which took the trophy.

A week later, and the hundred goals for the season was posted midway through an 8-1 thrashing of Ayr United, with, fittingly, a hat-trick for each of Gordon and O'Rourke, who had the lion's share of that total. Hibs went to Parkhead, for once confident of victory, but had to settle for a draw, and on New Year's Day they went to Tynecastle. Hibs won 7-0, and most doubted if they would see the side that would ever play anything like as well again. They didn't.

The celebrations lasted less than a week. East Fife came to Easter Road to defend, and they did so to such effect that it took a last-minute Gordon header to beat them. More significantly, John Brownlie broke his leg and was out for a year, and Alex Edwards eventually reacted to continual provocation, threw the

The Hibs' party celebrate their 1972 Drybrough Cup success. Back – W. Humphries, Cropley, T. McNiven, Edwards, Black, Gordon, Stanton, Schaedler. Front – Turnbull, Blackley, Hazel, Duncan, Brownlie, Hamilton, Herriott, with O'Rourke sitting on floor.

ball away, and was suspended for eight weeks for his fourth booking. It proved to be a turning point.

Hibs had drawn Hajduk Split in the Cupwinners Cup, reckoned a good draw, and Tom Hart spoke of taking Leeds in the final. Did this signify some complacency? Hibs set about their task at Easter Road with relish, Alan Gordon scored three of Hibs' four, but an enterprising attack got two back for the Yugoslavs. It was in Split that things went to pieces. The Hibs midfield seemed to have the game well in hand until two elementary and unusual errors by Herriot gave away two goals, and then in the second half, Blackley scored an own goal in trying to concede a corner.

Hibs had already lost interest in the Scottish Cup, losing a replay to Rangers after seeming to have done the difficult part by drawing at Ibrox, and that left only the league. That involvement lasted only four more days. Tommy McLean was a yard offside when he put Rangers ahead at Ibrox, and John Blackley was

Alan Gordon, elegant but
lethal centre of Turnbull's
Tornadoes of the early 70s.

Alan Gordon's header puts Hibs seven ahead in the 1973 Ne'erday derby.

John Brownlie lets fly at the Celtic goal at Parkhead in a league match, December 1972.

Kenny Garland (Hearts) thwarted Jimmy O'Rourke on this occasion in the 1973 New Year derby.

sent off for talking to a linesman about it. There was little sympathy for Blackley – he had been round long enough to know how often these things happened, but all of a sudden, as one commentator put it, Turnbull's Tornadoes had blown themselves out. Hibs finished the season with two cups, third in the league, with an enhanced reputation in Europe and totally deflated.

It was therefore important for them to bounce back quickly and reassert themselves, and this they did by winning the Drybrough Cup again in 1973. More importantly, they did it without Brownlie, and with youngsters Des Bremner, Tony Higgins and Iain Munro, a fine left-sided player signed from St Mirren. Alan Gordon scored the only goal of the final, in the last minute of extra time, to defy Celtic for the second year in succession.

For all that, Hibs failed too often to win the big games – Hearts took revenge for the January defeat with embarassing ease, and Hibs failed to even score in three games against Rangers – and by the end of the year the team was

McArthur, Brownlie and Schaedler guard the goalline against an incoming corner.

again on familiar lines, and only McArthur and Bremner were playing regularly who had not won league cupwinners' medals. Early in January, Hibs beat Hearts, East Fife and Dundee United in succession and slipped into second place in the table.

Joe Harper

IT WAS AT THE END OF THAT MONTH that manager Turnbull made his biggest and costliest mistake – the signing of Joe Harper from Everton. The fee was

Des Bremner is narrowly out of luck against Sochaux in a UEFA cup tie at Easter Road.

£120,000, or around half a million in today's terms, and easily a club record. Harper had failed to impress on Merseyside, but Turnbull clearly hoped that he could recapture the scoring touch which he had displayed when under Turnbull at Aberdeen. The now chubbier striker not only failed to live up to his expectation, but also to strike up any rapport with the Easter Road support, especially when it was seen that Jimmy O'Rourke was going to St. Johnstone to make way for him.

Hibs were already in debt, but were optimistic that the extra goals which would be forthcoming from their expensive buy would at last give them the edge to oust Celtic. The manager looked for gates averaging twenty thousand at Easter

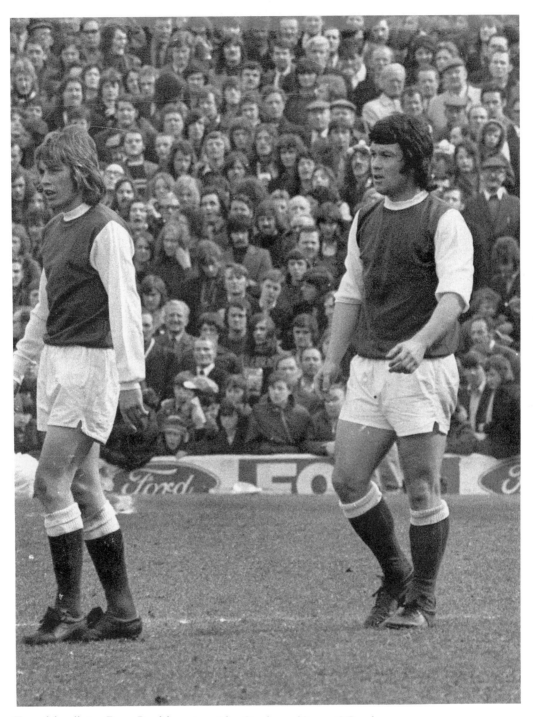

Two of the all time Easter Road favourites, Alex Cropley and Jimmy O'Rourke.

Derek Spalding (No. 5) and Tony Higgins against Rangers in the 1973 Drybrough Cup semi-final at Easter Road.

Road, and promised thrilling, entertaining play to attract them. Unfortunately these dreams were shattered in a single week as early as October – Celtic beating Hibs 5-0 in a league game, and 6-3 in the League Cup final, and Juventus scored four in a UEFA tie at Easter Road in midweek.

The turnaround in Hibs' fortunes can be traced to this period. The full cost of buying Harper became clearer when Alex Cropley, who had not asked for a transfer, was sold to Arsenal, although Ally McLeod, a skilful if enigmatic inside man, was brought from Southampton to take his place. When Alan Gordon, also

Eddie Turnbull's Hibs in the mid 70s. Back – Schaedler, Brownlie, O'Rourke, Munro, Murray, J. Fraser. Middle – W. Humphries, Higgins, Bremner, Smith, McArthur, Spalding, McGregor, Blackley, T. McNiven. Front – Duncan, Edwards, Gordon, Stanton, Harper, Cropley.

out of favour, joined Dundee a few weeks later, there was widespread discontent. The cavalier approach to the game was abandoned too, with one eye on the tighter competition of the forthcoming Premier League, and the resolve to present a harder target after the black week in October. Roy Barry, the former Hearts and Dunfermline stopper, was signed to add weight to the defence, and look after Dixie Deans. And despite all that had happened during the season, Hibs did edge out Celtic in the championship, only to find Rangers in front of both of them.

The effect was a sudden and dramatic alienation of supporters who came to be entertained by their favourites. Gates went down instead of up, and a stream of players left the club over the rest of the decade to make up for the loss of income at the turnstiles, a vicious spiral from which it was to take the club a considerable period to escape.

The entire Hibs squad parade their controversial Bukta strip with manager Eddie Turnbull. Season 1977–78.

A Hundred Years Of Hibs

RUNNERS-UP TWICE IN A ROW NOW, Hibs hoped for third time lucky – that they would be the first winners of the new Premier League, and in their centenary season too. Eddie Turnbull had been seriously ill, but came back for the centenary game against Brian Clough's Derby County in August 1975. The Englishmen won a rather undistinguished encounter by the only goal. Turnbull, however, was clearly not fully fit, and one of his priorities was to groom a successor.

In his condition, he was probably not the man to pour oil on the troubled waters within his charge. There was a row when Joe Harper turned up sporting a beard, and friction remained until Harper finally returned to Aberdeen late in

Harper leaves McGrain and Hunter helpless in the 1974 League Cup final against Celtic.

the season. Pat Stanton, asked to play among the forwards now to make up their lack of muscle, was made the scapegoat of a League Cup defeat at Montrose and amazingly omitted from Hibs' side set to defend a one-goal lead against Liverpool at Anfield. Alex Edwards was dropped after that tie and joined Stanton and the also dissatisfied John Blackley on the transfer list.

On the positive side, Hibs signed George Stewart, Mike McDonald and Ally Brazil during the season, the last-named a youngster who won under-21 honours and played for five Hibs' managers without ever quite having full backing from the terracing. But they also lost Iain Munro to Rangers, in exchange for Graham Fyfe and Ally Scott, supposedly the successor to Harper at centre.

By the start of season 1976-77, some of Turnbull's selections seemed bizarre, and there were more signs of discontent with the management. Stanton, Schaedler, Spalding and McLeod were all on the bench at one game on the Irish tour, and when McLeod was reinstated it was because Edwards was out of favour again.

Then in September came the announcement which was scarcely believable – a small crowd watched Hibs struggle to draw 0-0 with Montrose stunned by the news that Pat Stanton had gone to Celtic in exchange for Jackie McNamara, a 23-year-old inside forward who had failed to establish a first-team place at Parkhead.

Fewer than 10,000 fans watched Hibs against Sochaux in the UEFA Cup; the attack was Murray, Muir, Scott, Smith and Duncan and the only goal a fortuitous one from full back Brownlie. Hibs crashed out of the UEFA Cup in the second round somewhere in central Sweden, and only achieved their first home league win on Christmas Eve – a single goal against Ayr United before less than 4,000 spectators. They did not better that rally of one at Easter Road until they beat Kilmarnock 2-0 on March 9th, and that scarcely made up for the home defeat from Arbroath in the Cup. The attack had failed to average a goal a game for the first time, and depended on the experienced defence and seven points against Hearts to stay in the top league.

 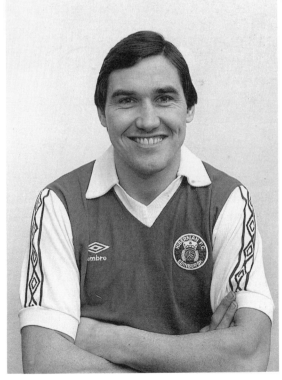

Two stars of the 70s – Ally McLeod, (left) top scorer five years in succession, and Jackie McNamara, who developed into a first class sweeper with Hibs.

A Purple Patch

WHAT WAS NEW IN 1977 was Hibs' sponsored jerseys. The Bukta logo was the first in the country, and the TV cameras, banned by Mr Hart from Easter Road in the past, now boycotted Hibs. A compromise was eventually reached where Hibs would wear un-logoed purple shirts when on TV, but as these clashed with Hearts, Rangers, Aberdeen and Dundee, they had to have yellow ones too.

Unfortunately, there was something of a "same again" look inside the new shirts, but efforts were made to improve the strike rate. Gordon Rae came from Whitehill with a bagful of goals, and went straight in to add power to the attack, but eventually found his best position further back. Jim McKay of Brora, and Rangers' Martin Henderson came on loan and went home. Then Erich Schaedler went to Dundee in exchange for striker Bobby Hutchinson, although it meant top scorer Bobby Smith going to full back to cover for Schaedler.

Gordon Rae gets in a flying header against Rangers at Easter Road. Picture courtesy of Ian Torrance.

There was also the move of John Blackley to Newcastle, to compensate for the problems of falling gates, and Bremner and Brazil were tried before McNamara made the sweeper position his. However, the new-look side, with the returns too of Brownlie and Higgins, suddenly hit upon the road to goal to such effect that they finally pipped Celtic for the final place in Europe, with a run which included a scintillating 4-1 thrashing of the Parkhead side.

Even in their quieter phases, Hibs were newsworthy, courtesy of their ebullient chairman. In the past Mr Hart had commented on the cowardice of the Old Firm in failing to play each other, and the butchery of Bristol City in recent years, but in 1978 he was after bigger fish. Supported by no less dogged a campaigner than Tam Dalyell, still free of General Belgrano concerns, Hart took on the Department

Manchester United came to Easter Road to make use of the new undersoil heating on Boxing Day 1980. Ralph Callachan (above) helped Hibs hold them to 1-1.

of Employment over the refusal to grant work permits to Refvik and Mathiesen, two Norwegians whom Hibs had signed. It was no easy task, given the determinedly out-of-touch stance of the Employment Secretary Albert Booth, and the two Scandinavians were long gone before the rules were finally changed, to the benefit of many Scottish sides since.

Meanwhile, without reaching the greatest of heights, Hibs had their best season for some time, which softened the blow of John Brownlie going to Newcastle. With four games left, they were level on points with Aberdeen, Morton and St. Mirren for fourth place, but finally missed a UEFA place. They also reached the Cup Final, where their titanic struggle with Rangers over 330 minutes ended tragically with Arthur Duncan's own goal. Two notable opponents in the cup run were Steve Archibald, who scored Aberdeen's semi-final goal, and Alex Miller, who missed a penalty for Rangers in the final.

If Hibs' prolonged endeavours in the cup came as a pleasant surprise, then it was not long before they seemed as distant as last year's holidays. Survival in the Premier Division depended on making the most of home advantage and trying to sneak away points, and Hibs failed to do both. With home defeats from Rangers and Celtic early on, they were cut adrift from the pack with only five games gone.

It was clear that a great deal was being asked of Des Bremner in midfield – just how much was evident after he was transferred to Aston Villa in September 1979 for £220,000 plus Joe Ward, the former Clyde striker. Ward joined other new men Whyte, Reid, Rodier and Docherty at Easter Road, and made no more of an impression. It was assumed that Jim Brown, the ex-Hearts captain who had crossed the city during the summer, would take over Bremner's mantle.

George Best

BY NOVEMBER, Hibs were firmly rooted in the basement, and in need of a lift, and it came with the improbable signing of George Best, back from America and on the lookout for a club. The idea was first mooted by the *Evening News*, and followed up by Messrs Hart and Turnbull, and Best first turned out in a Hibs jersey at Love Street in December.

Best came into the sterile world of the Premier League like a ray of sunshine, albeit a late evening one. For his home debut, against those most uncharismatic of opponents Partick Thistle, the crowd exceeded 22,000, and nearly doubled that of the league cup semi-final at Hampden the same day. Throughout his stay, large crowds turned out every time Best did, or when they thought he would.

In many ways, however, the move failed. Best's aim was to sell himself to an English First Division club, Hibs's target was to win points and avoid the drop,

George Best added some welcome sparkle to the unhappy relegation season of 1979–80.

and neither was close to being achieved. Best's skill on the ball diverted attention from reality, which was that of a once-great player, separated from his greatness by many years of bad living, playing for a poor team stranded at the bottom of the league. In total, Best played around twenty-five games for Hibs, scored four goals, and three times let the club down by failing to appear.

By early 1980, the fight for top league status was as good as lost, but Hibs did keep some interest alive by reaching the Scottish Cup semi-finals, helped by successive draws against Meadowbank, Ayr and Berwick. The 5-0 thrashing by Celtic at that stage proved the final straw for Eddie Turnbull – and Tom Hart – and a few days later Turnbull was sacked as Hibs' manager, and removed from the board. Turnbull in any case had come to hate the pressures of the Premier League, and had been set the task some years earlier of grooming a successor. Ironically, at the same time, Gordon Strachan, whom Turnbull had let go some years earlier, was voted "Player of the Year".

There were three main candidates for the job – Willie Ormond, who had been abruptly dismissed by Hearts early the same year and who had assisted Turnbull since, Pat Stanton, who had recently resigned as Aberdeen assistant manager to return to Edinburgh, and Peter Cormack, who had returned to Easter Road as player in March, to be groomed for management. It was Ormond who was given a two-year contract to bring Hibs back up in one season, and he started by handing out twelve free transfers.

After a distinguished career with Hibs in the Fifties, Willie Ormond succeeded his old team mate Eddie Turnbull, as manager.

CHAPTER 8

The Eighties

ANY FEARS THAT HIBS would find the going hard in the First Division proved groundless. At the start of the season, their main rivals seemed to be Dundee, Ayr United and Motherwell, and when Hibs beat all three in a single week in October, the path to promotion seemed clear. George Best put in a series of farewell appearances, and with players like McLeod, Callaghan and John Connolly from Everton, Hibs simply had too much class for their opponents. Of the younger brigade, Craig Paterson and Gordon Rae promised most.

It was important that Hibs made their mark early on, because with the campaign barely a third gone, Willie Ormond resigned in poor health. This time Tom Hart gave the job to Bertie Auld, currently boss at Partick Thistle, and doubtless with an eye for the forthcoming fight for survival in the Premier League. For that struggle, Auld signed Alan Sneddon from Celtic for £60,000, since proven a very good buy, and the strong-running Gary Murray from Montrose, who never quite hit it off in the top flight, for a similar sum. Hibs cruised uneventfully to the First Division title, with a club record points total and a 2-0 win over Raith, the only side to give them any trouble in the race for points, to clinch it.

A season in the First Division cost Hibs dear, and these problems were not entirely dismissed on their move back up; Bertie Auld's Partick Thistle had never been noted for playing with gay abandon, and while it was appreciated with Auld in charge, the spectre of relegation was more or less banished, fewer and fewer supporters were turning out to see the wars of attrition which were keeping the club in mid-table. There was also the matter of Craig Paterson going to Rangers – neither Paterson nor Hibs were in any position to resist the terms offered, but it didn't help at the turnstiles.

Meanwhile, behind the scenes, Tom Hart was getting close to calling it a day, and in October 1981, Kenny Waugh, a local businessman with bookmaking and other leisure interests, was co-opted to the board, with a view to buying Hart out in the near future. Waugh had had a taste for football with an abortive attempt to buy Hearts in the summer, although his affections had always lain at Easter Road. Hart continued to speak his mind as always, and he was fined by the SFA for suggesting that a Rangers' player had conned the referee into awarding a

Alan Sneddon, an excellent signing by Bertie Auld, seen in action, along with David Fellenger, against Dundee in 1989–90.

penalty – hard to believe, isn't it? A few weeks later, Hibs' extrovert chairman collapsed at Pittodrie, and died in an Aberdeen hospital.

So after a long spell of continuity, things changed fast at Easter Road. Waugh took over somewhat earlier than intended, which resulted in a new board, although Hart's son Alan remained for some years. By the autumn, with Paterson away, attendances falling further as the fans refused to pay for the style of football provided, and morale generally low, Waugh sacked Bertie Auld as an "economy measure". Although Auld, and Pat Quinn his assistant, had both played for Hibs, Waugh believed that supporters would rally round a club with which they could identify, and Pat Stanton, manager of Dunfermline by now, was installed the same day, with Jimmy O'Rourke and George Stewart as assistants.

Pat Stanton

KENNY WAUGH may have given Hibs' fans the manager they could believe in, but he scarcely gave him the tools to do the job. It is a general business truth that one has to invest to earn a return, and with the goals in football essentially short-term ones, for a football club in trouble, that means buying players. Waugh

Willie Irvine, a prolific goalscorer for Hibs in the early 1980s.

Alan Rough, a major signing by Pat Stanton, at the time Scotland's most capped goalkeeper.

The Hibs' squad under Pat Stanton and John Blackley. Can you spot the youthful Mickey Weir, Paul Kane and Gordon Hunter?

Kenny Waugh, chairman from 1980 to 1987.

tended to take the opposite view; Hibs were losing money, so expenditure was cut to meet income, which brought about lower gates and less income. The ultimate outcome is inescapable.

Pat Stanton was amazed at the decline in the club in the few years since he had left, but with the necessary cash not forthcoming, could only sign Mike Conroy, a Celtic reserve player, and Willie Irvine, who came from Motherwell as a swap for Bobby Flavell, who had come to Hibs on a free transfer earlier. Late in 1982, money was found to buy Alan Rough from Partick Thistle, a lifesaving signing if ever there was one, but so short-handed were Hibs elsewhere that Graham Harvey went straight into the first team from Ormiston Primrose.

The human touch provided by the new management team enabled a happier atmosphere to prevail than previously, and Hibs finished seventh in the league, which seemed to confirm to the board that nothing further was needed. But there were other problems too, notably the manager being bypassed altogether on occasion, and towards the end of the season, Stanton resigned. He was

'Kano' signed by Bertie Auld was introduced to the first team by Pat Stanton.

persuaded to return, but Jimmy O'Rourke and George Stewart had had enough, and both left at the end of the season.

John Blackley, at the time with Hamilton, became Stanton's new assistant, and had to help out on the pitch too. Bobby Thomson, a player with a wild reputation, was signed from Middlesbrough, and for half a season his engagement of the opposition created the space for Irvine to notch a score of goals.

Unfortunately, in December 1983, Thomson went over the score and assaulted a linesman, and was suspended for six months, effectively ending his career with Hibs, and Willie Irvine's goalscoring.

Nevertheless, the pressure from a support so bereft of goals for so long persuaded chairman and manager to offer Irvine an excessive contract to keep him from going to Tynecastle, especially in a summer which saw moves for Tommy McQueen of Clyde and Jamie Doyle of Partick Thistle fail, and the cash to buy East Fife's Gordon Durie unavailable.

The long-term prospects were brighter, however, and good youngsters were again coming onstream. Bertie Auld had taken Hibs into the professional youth league with considerable success, and it seemed that better things were in store if Hibs could ride out present difficulties. Brian Rice, Paul Kane, Gordon Hunter, Michael Weir and John Collins were to make the grade, and Kevin McKee showed promise until his confidence went after being attacked on the Ibrox pitch.

Stanton remained unhappy with his board, and things came to a head in September. First there was the upsetting McKee incident, and then Stanton was fined £500 for questioning one of Brian McGinlay's wrong decisions at Pittodrie. This fine was announced at about the same time as the thug who attacked McKee was fined £100, and confirmed to Stanton the quality of justice to which he had been subjected. Although it was so early in the season, there was a "relegation" battle at home to Dumbarton, and Hibs lost 3-2. Disillusioned and frustrated, Pat Stanton resigned.

John Blackley

JOHN BLACKLEY was appointed caretaker manager while the position was advertised – and Billy McNeill of Manchester City headhunted, it was believed – and the performances were such that he was offered the permanent position. "Permanent" is of course used in the sense unique to football club management jobs. This time £65,000 was found to buy Gordon Durie, and Tommy Craig, the

A fine study of Gordon Durie, now of Chelsea, of whose game long throw-ins were a prominent feature.

ex-Aberdeen player, became Blackley's assistant. He too was called upon for service on the field before long.

Blackley's main task was to avoid the drop (yet again), this time a two-horse race with Dumbarton to avoid ninth place. By January, Dumbarton were five points ahead, and their manager was talking about the issue being settled before the final meeting of the teams. Hibs had much the better squad on paper, but it only showed after they finally got a break, and two unexpected points, at Ibrox. They beat Celtic too, and another new signing, Joe McBride, brought them back from the dead with two late late goals at Tynecastle. Hibs beat Dumbarton in their fourth meeting with confidence and ease, and finished with eight points more than the Sons.

It was in 1985 that a major initiative was taken at Easter Road: Kenny Waugh brought in three new directors, Gregor Cowan, Alan Young and Jack Douglas, and hired Raymond Sparkes as a Marketing Manager. Gordon Neely was brought in to coach the young players. Major ground improvements were undertaken, with the main terracing decapitated and covered.

There was also some cash for players, although most of that came from Nottingham Forest, whom a tribunal ordered to pay £175,000 for Brian Rice. Steve Cowan from Aberdeen, Mark Fulton from Hamilton and Gordon Chisholm from Sunderland were added to the pool, but Hibs' first league win did not come until the end of September, by which time they were bottom.

The Skol Cup was something else. Hibs hit six against both Cowdenbeath and Motherwell, mainly because of the new striking partnership of Cowan and Durie, and then beat Celtic on penalties after a 4-4 draw which was as exciting as anyone could remember. Chisholm scored a debut goal to help Hibs oust Rangers in the two-legged semi-final, and even if Hibs were somewhat outclassed by Aberdeen in the final, it was a fine achievement to get there.

League form perked up too, at least to the point where survival was assured, and there was another extended run in the spring, in the Scottish Cup. There was another titanic struggle with Celtic, which Hibs won 4-3 after being down 2-1 with just fifteen minutes to go. Again Hibs ran into a brick wall in the guise of Aberdeen, this time at the semi-final stage. In retrospect, however, the cup runs tended to cloud the issue that the league season had been poor, before petering out altogether, there seemed to be tension behind the scenes again, and the unhappy Durie went to Chelsea before it finished for more than six times what he had cost.

For 1986-87, Blackley bought no fewer than five new players with the cash. The Dundee United pair Kirkwood and Beedie cost £150,000, and chairman Waugh went halfway round the world to sign Mark Caughey at Northern Ireland's World Cup base in Arizona. George McCluskey, the veteran ex-Celt, and another Willie Irvine, from Stirling Albion, were the others.

John Blackley and Alex Ferguson lead their teams on to Hampden Park for the 1985 League Cup final.

August 1986 and flashpoint at Easter Road – Graeme Souness' humiliating dismissal in the first half of his Premier League debut. George McCluskey and Billy Kirkwood do little to console the Rangers' boss.

The season got off to an explosive start, against Rangers in their first game with Butcher and Co, under Graeme Souness. Souness lasted only 37 minutes when he was sent off for two dreadful tackles, and his victim, McCluskey, missed several games. Hibs won 2-1, but thereafter seemed no better than before, with their much-vaunted new players generally disappointing. Only three victories were recorded in seventeen games, rumours abounded about ill-feeling within Easter Road, and after a particularly insipid performance by his team at Paisley, John Blackley joined a growing list of Hibs ex-managers.

Steve Cowan expresses his delight about scoring against Falkirk.

Brian Rice left Hibs to join Nottingham Forest. The fee of £200,000 had to be settled by tribunal.

John Collins, now displaying his considerable skills with Celtic.

Alex Miller

THIS TIME THE APPOINTMENT OF A NEW MANAGER was not kept within the club. Tommy Craig had been the caretaker while the job was advertised, but even Hamilton had won easily at Easter Road, and Craig ended up assisting Billy McNeil with Celtic. Alex Miller was appointed to the Hibs post – he was already manager of St. Mirren, but saw Hibs as much the bigger club. Miller had to live with his long playing career at Ibrox, but his commitment to Hibs was clear from the moment he took over. Moreover, he brought former favourite Peter Cormack back to be his assistant.

A change of managers is often associated with a good run of results, but in Miller's case, Hibs failed to score in five games. It took a triple signing on Hogmanay for Hibs to turn the corner, a win at Falkirk and as exciting an Edinburgh derby as one could wish – Dougie Bell (Rangers), Tommy McIntyre (Aberdeen) and Graham Mitchell (Hamilton) were all bought on the one day, and gradually Kirkwood, Fulton, Beedie, Irvine and Caughey went elsewhere.

It was not long before Hibs seemed to be taking shape in the way that the new manager wanted, although there was no sudden transformation in results. It was not even certain until late on the Hibs would avoid the three relegation places – the Premier League was in a peculiar state of reconstruction – and they were bustled out of the cup by Clydebank just a week after beating them 4-1 in the league. Season 1986-87 therefore did not live up to the optimism with which it started, but there was fresh hopes for its successor.

It has been a feature of Alex Miller's tenure of office that progress has been steady rather than spectacular. Many good players have come to this club, the manager has been tireless in his pursuit of good youngsters and the club has certainly been less concerned about relegation that before, having moved up one step towards having Europe as a realistic aim. This has been easier in recent times, of course, with the exclusion of English sides and the success of Dundee United and Aberdeen making five places for Scottish sides. But despite having the best squad of players for a long time, Hibs have yet to mount a consistent challenge to the top four.

The events surrounding the club have been more dramatic than the achievements of the team in recent times. This started in the summer of 1987, when, after negotiations lasting several weeks, Kenny Waugh sold his stake in Hibs to David Duff, who had been brought up a Hibs supporter in Trinity, but was unknown in local circles. His family had moved south, and Duff was now Swindon-based, a lawyer with other interests in property and leisure. At 33, he also became Hibs' youngest chairman. Jim Gray, Duff's bother-in-law, was brought in from managing a construction company to be managing director, and a "new tomorrow" was promised. To show immediate good intent, Neil Orr was bought from West Ham for £100,000, and made a scoring debut against Queen of the South.

Changes came thick and fast. Hibs were to be more widely based than just a football club in future, and Scotland's first female club director, Sheila Rowland, was added to the board, as well as Jeremy James, both with experience in the property sector. Raymond Sparkes, who had earlier left the Waugh camp, returned to revitalise the commercial side of the enterprise. On the playing side there was a blow when Mickey Weir walked out on Hibs and joined Luton, but four months later he came back. Alex Miller was probably disappointed at the time when Ian Andrews, the England under-21 goalkeeper declined to join Hibs,

An incredible goal! Gordon Hunter, Gordon Rae and Steve Archibald have all hit the bar within a few seconds, and the ball falls for Paul Kane to crash it into the roof of the net for Hibs' opening goal against Motherwell.

Eddie May, Paul Kane, Steve Cowan, Mickey Weir and Tommy McIntyre congratulate John Collins on his goal that beat Rangers 1-0 at Easter Road in August 1987.

Neil Orr's determined run leaves this opponent trailing.

until, that is, he got Andy Goram from Oldham for £325,000. And later in the season Gareth Evans came from Rotherham, and scored in his first appearance against Dundee.

The actual football was less memorable; Hibs played in fits and starts and finished seventh in the table. Soccer hooliganism reached new levels of idiocy when a can of anti-riot gas was thrown from the Celtic section of Easter Road onto the main terraces, causing considerable panic and about a hundred and forty injuries. Andy Goram collapsed after a clash at Ibrox, and apparently might have died because referee Kenny Hope thought it more important to follow the law than allow him attention. Fortunately Goram recovered to finish the season on a lighter note by scoring in the last game against Morton.

The focus was off football again in the autumn of 1988, when Hibs became the first Scottish club to have its shares traded on the Stock Exchange. Hibs were to be one of three subsidiaries of Edinburgh Hibernian plc, whose other

Graham Mitchell shows the determination which characterises his game.

Callum Milne follows every move of Hearts' John Colquhoun, while Gordon Hunter covers.

branches were to be involved in property and leisure, to generate the long-term finance which would, it was hoped, enable Hibs to be able to compete with the Old Firm on economic grounds. Despite an IBA ban on the proposed issue, the 30% of the shares offered to the public were avidly taken up at 55p, and later traded at around 75p on the secondary market.

The preoccupation with money about this time was scarcely diminished by the arrival of Steve Archibald, who had fallen out of favour with Barcelona. Archibald provided some class on the pitch when he was there, but the frequent disputes about his contract, transfer requests and his example of walking out when not selected were not constructive. Money always seemed to be at the root of the problem, to the extent that when John Collins was showered with coins by Hearts fans, a club official thought that Archibald would be in there checking the denominations. Archibald finally found what he wanted, a pot of gold, and set out for the Spanish second division side which promised it.

There was considerable optimism when Hibs made what appeared to be an

The Hibs' squad who won the 1990 Tennents Sixes in such style. Andy Goram captained the team and Paul Kane (3rd from left) was the competition's top scorer.

ambitious signing, and Archibald was the club's top scorer with fifteen goals. By December, attendances at Easter Road were up by more than a quarter, as Hibs challenged for their first European place for eleven years, essentially a two-horse race with St. Mirren, and reached the Scottish Cup semi-finals. Yet more ambition was shown in signing Keith Houchen, the big strong Coventry striker, for £300,000, even if they failed to bring Newcastle's Irish midfielder Michael O'Neill to Easter Road as well. Houchen also got off to the best of starts with a spectacular headed goal at Tynecastle.

Another major signing, in the summer of 1989, was Brian Hamilton from St. Mirren for a similar sum; this was financed largely from the sale of Eddie May

Andy Goram, Gordon Hunter and Joe Tortolano combine to keep out Rangers' Terry Butcher, with Gareth Evans looking on.

Gordon Hunter has trouble getting away from John Robertson of Hearts. Billy Kirkwood is the other Hibs' man in the picture.

Mickey Weir and Rangers' Butch Wilkins vie for possession at Easter Road, with Ian Ferguson and Graham Mitchell poised to assist.

to Brentford and the fine on Andy Goram for playing cricket against orders. At least this season the talk was all about football, and especially the UEFA Cup, for many supporters their first taste of European football. Those who travelled to Hungary saw a performance that any of Hibs' earlier European teams would have been proud of, and got a taste of Eastern Europe before its traumatic transformation. The thousands who went to Liège impressed by their noise and behaviour, and saw their favourites beaten only by a freak goal in extra time.

The spring of 1990 was the most frustrating period; without ever being in the driving seat, Hibs were never out of the running for a UEFA Cup place, and one of the uncertainties was just how many such places there would be for Scottish clubs. This seemed to depend largely on the performance of English fans in Italy. To mount their challenge, Hibs bought Paul Wright, the ex-Aberdeen striker, from Queens Park Rangers, and the teenage Mark McGraw, whose father had also played for Hibs, from Morton. The optimism that these moves inspired did not last long – McGraw damaged ligaments the same day as Brian Hamilton broke a leg at Ibrox, and a week later, Wright, after just one full game, was sidelined for the rest of the season by a crude challenge by Hearts' Neil Berry.

Nevertheless, after beating Rangers and Aberdeen, six points from their last six games – or possibly five – would have done, but Hibs managed only four, and in the last three games failed to win against teams below them. Indeed, with a few minutes to go in their final game at Dunfermline, Hibs were still playing for fourth place, yet despite losing neither the game nor even another goal, and earning as near to a good press as they had all season, they finished seventh, behind not only Dundee United and Celtic who were also in contention for a European place, but also Motherwell who were not. And to cap it all, John Collins of all people missed a penalty in the last minute of his last appearance at Easter Road against Dundee.

Paul Wright, pictured on signing for Hibs.

Mark McGraw, signed from Morton. Mark's father Alan also played for Hibs.

Brian Hamilton, signed from St. Mirren and doing well for Hibs in mid-field.

Murdo MacLeod has just signed for Hibernian. Alex Miller looks on approvingly.

PART THREE
Past Masters

Willie Groves

"**D**ARLING WILLIE" GROVES was Edinburgh football's most romantic and tragic character of its early years. No one so captured the affections of the Hibs support of the nineteenth century, and, like only Joe Baker in 1961, although he left the club not long out of his teens, he never lost it.

Groves is not a Scottish name; it arrived in Edinburgh when a London police sergeant was seconded to the Edinburgh force to help solve a series of crimes which culminated in the arrest of Deacon Brodie. His grandson, Patrick William, was born in Glasgow in August 1868.

Willie grew up in Edinburgh, and his first club was Thistle, from whom he joined Hibs towards the end of season 1885-86. Hibs were already the top side in the area, and Groves' skill and flair added just what was needed to win the Scottish Cup and unofficial world championship. "No more fascinating player ever appeared in a football arena. Tall, sinewy and graceful, on the ball his work was beautifully close, artful and deceptive. He was a picturesque figure, a sort of Romeo in the sport with his raven locks and classic cut features." Groves' speed and swerve made him often seem unstoppable, and it was one of his thrilling solo runs which set up Hibs' winner in the 1887 Scottish Cup final. He earned his first Scottish cap the following season while still a teenager.

But Groves also had a commercial side to his nature, and he joined Celtic at its inception in 1888, making his enduring popularity in the capital all the more remarkable. He next signed for Everton, but did not play for the Anfield club, then moved to West Bromwich in 1890, and Aston Villa in 1893. While in England, he picked up an FA Cup winners' medal with West Brom and a League Champions' badge with Villa two years later: he played in the first-ever league international – for England against Scotland.

Even by the mid-1890s, with Groves still in his twenties, his health began to fail. He returned to Edinburgh and rejoined Hibs in time to play in the 1896 Scottish Cup final against Hearts, without recapturing the form of earlier years. A year or two later, he returned south of the border, in comparatively modest company, and soon had to finish his career. He returned again to Edinburgh, where he lingered rather than lived, now a widower, until his death, from heart disease, in February 1909 and at 39 years of age, in Longmore Hospital, Newington.

Harry Rennie

HENRY GEORGE, or "Harry G.", Rennie was not the only best goalkeeper in Britain during the early part of the century, but was also one of Scottish football's greatest characters.

Rennie came from Greenock, and played minor and junior football in the area until he signed for Morton. In those days he was a half-back and was capped as an outfield player by the Scottish Junior FA while with Greenock West End.

It was only in 1897, around his twenty-fourth birthday, Harry Rennie became a goalkeeper, for which he immediately demonstrated a natural and unique talent. It was unique for one thing inasmuch as he spent much of his time playing a modern "sweeper" role far from his goal. Rennie was also the first goalkeeper to mark out his goal area as an aid to his positioning. His ability was soon recognised too; in 1898 he left Morton for Hearts, and won his first two caps in 1899-1900 with the Tynecastle team.

Celtic next showed an interest, but there was a mix-up concerning the transfer to Parkhead and Hibs stepped in. Another feature of Harry Rennie was that he was the first player to write his own contract and present it to the club to sign, and it may be that Hibs were more willing to meet the player's terms than the other two.

However it was achieved, Hibs had acquired a personality and a star, who stayed for eight years; he won a further 11 caps and 7 league cups, and a cup and league badge with Hibs, and was as responsible as anyone for Hibs' successes at the turn of the century. He was also a close friend of Bobby Walker of Hearts, and the two had a sizeable bet on whether the Hearts man would score each time they met in a derby game.

In 1908, Rennie left Hibs for Rangers, and got a cup-finalists' medal for the 1909 final when the cup was withheld after a riot. Short spells in Inverness and Kilmarnock finished off an unusual career.

A final feature of Harry Rennie was his almost disfigured look in most photographs: this was caused by an early encounter with a cricket ball. Eventually Rennie had the injured jaw rectified, luckily after he left Hibs, because reports are that he was never again the same goalkeeper.

Willie Harper

WILLIE HARPER was the Hibs goalkeeper of the twenties, an internationalist and simply the best of his day. He was a big, strong athletic player, and during his wartime service with the Scots Guards and the Royal Flying Corps, played championship football and rugby, won the Scots Guards' heavyweight boxing title, and helped the airmen's team to tug-of-war honours.

Harper was born in Winchburgh, in West Lothian, in 1897, and played locally while he served his time as a blacksmith's apprentice at Winchburgh Oil Works before joining the Edinburgh junior side Emmett, shortly after hostilities ended in 1918. He only played seven or eight games before Barney Lester, Hibs director, spotted him, and he joined up at Easter Road in 1920.

Harper brought a security to the Easter Road back division which had not been evident since Rennie had left, and recognition was not long in coming; he was capped against England in 1923 in the first international at Wembley and became a fixture in the Scotland side during the rest of his stay with Hibs. He played against England four times and was never on the losing side; he also won three league caps, and he played in the 1923 and 1924 Scottish Cup finals.

With Scotland having such supremacy over the Auld Enemy, it was inevitable that English cheque books should be brought north, and most of the national eleven were transferred to English clubs. In Harper's case it was Arsenal who bought his services, and Hibs were compensated by £5,000, then a world record transfer fee for a goalkeeper.

Unfortunately, things did not work out for Harper in London. He won just one more cap, in two spells made fewer than a hundred appearances for the Gunners and in 1927 emigrated to Fall River in the United States. He was not able to settle there, however, and three years later he returned to England and to Arsenal, before being transferred to Plymouth Argyle in December 1931.

Harper evidently found the West Country more to his liking, because more than half a century later he was still with Argyle; he had retired in the mid thirties to the backroom staff, although he did make a few appearances when over forty. He served Plymouth in almost every backroom capacity over the years, and was rewarded with a benefit against Arsenal in 1972; three years later he was the oldest surviving player at the Hibs' centenary dinner.

Jimmy Dunn

JIMMY DUNN was an outstanding example of a Scottish inside forward of his time – small, tricky and tenatious. He was a member of the memorable Hibs' team of the nineteen twenties, and achieved a permanent place in Scottish footballing lore by being one of the famous "Wembley Wizards".

Dunn was a Glaswegian, and was spotted after the First World War with the junior outfit St. Anthony's, practically all of whose team of around 1920 went to Celtic. To the journalists of the west of Scotland, he was generally referred to as Tim. At Easter Road, Dunn quickly formed a formidable right-wing partnership with the popular Harry Ritchie; they both won international recognition, and played together in the consecutive Scottish Cup finals of 1923 and 1924.

Apart from being capable of some bewildering footwork, Dunn was possessed of a deceptively powerful shot for such a frail-looking man of only five foot six inches, and he became the second player, after Jimmy McColl, to register a century of league and cup goals for Hibs. That was in 1928, which was an unforgettable year for Jimmy Dunn – it was in March of that year that he took part in Scotland's 5-1 thrashing of England at Wembley, and during the summer, he and Ritchie were transferred to Everton.

Things were not dull on Merseyside; in successive seasons, Dunn experienced the disappointment of relegation, a second division winner's medal, a first division winner's medal and an FA Cupwinner's badge. That was won in the 1933 competition, where Dunn was one of the scorers against a Manchester City eleven which included Matt Busby.

In his mid-thirties, Exeter City paid a club record fee to attract Dunn to St. James' Park, and he ended a fine career as player-manager of non-league Runcorn. He had won six full caps, and had one league international appearance to his credit. Dunn died in 1963. He had a son, also Jimmy, who also won an FA Cup winner's medal, with Wolverhampton Wanderers, in 1949.

Gordon Smith

I REMEMBER AS A BOY hearing my father saying that Gordon Smith was as skilful as Stanley Matthews and as good a goalscorer as Tom Finney. I thought then that he was completely over the top, but I was wrong.

Smith was born in Edinburgh, in 1924, but grew up an exiled Hearts supporter in Montrose. He came to prominence as a centre-forward, scoring a hat-trick for a Dundee junior select against a Hearts-Hibs XI, and, with both Edinburgh sides after him, was persuaded to sign for Hibs in April 1941, for the princely sum of £10. On his debut he scored a hat-trick against Hearts at Tynecastle.

By the end of the war, Smith was an internationalist, and had a century of goals in the Scottish Southern League to his credit. The goalscoring continued, and virtually every record for a winger went his way – five goals in a game against Third Lanark, a further century of Scottish League goals, and a career total of 364 goals, the fifth highest of any player in Scotland. Gordon Smith is usually recalled as the outstanding member of the famous front line of the '50s, but many who saw him earlier maintain that he was even better in the '40s.

He took over the club captaincy of Hibs from Davie Shaw in 1949, and skippered his country too, on the successful European tour of 1955. Until then, he had always felt that he was not considered a first choice for Scotland, which may explain why his most memorable performances were in green and white. In all Smith played 18 times for his country, as well as gaining 9 caps for the Scottish League.

In 1958, Smith had ankle trouble, missing the cup final that year, and a year later required an operation on the same joint; by this time he was thirty-five, but Hibs refused to pay the bill, and he was freed. The player had the operation at his own expense and proved himself right by going on to win league championship medals with Hearts and Dundee. He also represented both clubs in the European Cup, and his record of having played for three clubs in Europe's premier competition is the more remarkable for his being over thirty when the competition started.

Gordon Smith finally retired after twenty-three years in top-grade football, fitting reward for healthy living, and now lives quietly near North Berwick.

Lawrie Reilly

LAWRIE REILLY is synonymous with the golden period of Hibernian history after the second World War, as the leader of the Famous Five attack, and Scotland's first-choice centre for many years. A superb opportunist with head and either foot, Reilly was also a versatile footballer – he joined Hibs as an outside-right and was capped as an outside-left before becoming a centre – and developed into an accomplished attack leader.

Reilly grew up in Edinburgh, but uncomfortably near Tynecastle Park, so that when in addition he started work as an apprentice painter for his uncle, a Hearts' shareholder whose business was based in Gorgie Road, Lawrie's goalscoring exploits for the Edinburgh Thistle juvenile side quickly reached the wrong ears. Fortunately, Reilly's father was a Hibs supporter, and Thistle were run by Harry Reading, Hibs' groundsman who directed so many fine players to Easter Road, and swift action by these two brought Willie McCartney at the double to sign him.

Reilly was only sixteen then, but when peacetime football resumed, he was in the Hibs reserve side which was almost unbeatable. He made several first-team appearances, but his longest run was when Willie Ormond broke his leg in 1948; Reilly made such a good job of deputising that he was capped for Scotland in Cardiff at outside-left, and, later in the season, when Ormond came back but

Alex Linwood had gone to Clyde, Reilly took over at centre, and never looked back.

Reilly was already a fixture in the Scotland team to the extent that he won thirty-eight caps during the next eight years, and despite a serious bout of pleurisy in 1954, which kept him out of the World Cup. He scored 22 goals, at a faster rate than Law or Dalglish, and scored five goals in five appearances at Wembley, including the famous last-minute equaliser in 1953. He also restricted such a rival as Willie Bauld (Hearts) to three caps. When Bobby Johnstone came into the attack, Hibs had the best front line in the country, and Reilly was the Division A's top scorer three times in succession, one admittedly jointly.

Reilly was ill for most of 1954, but after returning in October, was back in the Scottish side to play England in the spring of 1955. His career for his country ended at Wembley two years later, and, bothered by knee trouble too by now, Reilly was forced to call it a day with a memorable final game for Hibs against Rangers in April 1958.

These days, Lawrie still runs his hostelry in Leith, and plays golf to a good standard, as well as running the ex-Hibernian players' golf club.

Joe Baker

NO MORE EXPLOSIVE TALENT ever hit the Scottish goal scene than Joe Baker, and just at the right time to take over from the departing Lawrie Reilly. Baker was a two-footed centre and superb in the air, a rare combination, and these talents were allied to a pace and aggression in his hunger for goals that was at times breathtaking. A measure of the impact that he made as a youngster is that he became the first player from a club outwith England ever to be capped for that country, and he did so while still a teenager. Joe's only regret about it all was that it was England he was eligible for and not Scotland.

Baker was born in Liverpool in 1940, but six weeks later he was brought to Motherwell to escape the bombing. He was a stand-out in schools football, scoring five times for Lanarkshire schools against Edinburgh at Tynecastle, then both for Scottish Schools in a 2-2 draw against England at Goodison Park. Chelsea took him south as a fifteen-year-old, but Baker was homesick and soon came north, where Hibs' scout Davie Wyper befriended him, and made sure Hibs would benefit from his talent.

Farmed out to Armadale for a year, Baker was called up to Easter Road in 1957, and within a month he had made his debut for the first team. His first goal was in a 4-2 win at Tynecastle to hansel Hearts' new floodlights, and a few months later, in an amazing cup tie at the same venue, Baker scored four goals to send the league leaders tumbling out of the cup. Two more followed against Third Lanark in the quarter finals, and, with Reilly having to call it a day in April 1958, Baker was a regular while still only seventeen.

In the following two seasons, Baker averaged more than a goal a game, and the spells in which he played alongside Gordon Smith and Bobby Johnstone suggested a few "might-have-beens" if he had received that kind of support regularly. As it was, Baker scored 42 league goals in 1959-60, to keep a side which lost 2.5 goals a game in the top half of the table. He also ousted Brian Clough from the England No. 9 shirt, and won a clutch of honours at under-23 and full international level.

Wider attention came with his displays against Barcelona and Roma, and when Baker was put on the transfer list against his wishes for asking for a rise, it was Torino who secured his signature. Joe had one year in Italy, and that was a nightmare, with a horrific car crash, two suspensions, legal trouble with a photographer and eventually the cancellation of his contract. He was glad to return to Britain, and spent the rest of the 'sixties with Arsenal, Nottingham Forest and Sunderland. It was from Roker Park that Hibs brought Baker back to Edinburgh, and an emotional second debut win against Eddie Turnbull's Aberdeen.

Dave Ewing was in charge at that time, and when Eddie Turnbull took over soon after, things did not work out as hoped. A lingering injury kept Baker out for months, Turnbull bought Alan Gordon, and Baker went to Raith Rovers. After retiring, Joe had five years as a publican, and then spent some time in the ice-cream trade before entering the construction industry. He has always wanted to use his wealth of experience in football in a managerial capacity, but while he has been in charge of mainly junior clubs, he has always found it frustrating that a break in the major game has not come his way; currently, however, Joe is coaching Albion Rovers, under Davie Provan, and was a major factor in that club's promotion to the First Division in 1989.

Pat Stanton

THERE ARE MANY DISTINCTIVE FEATURES about Pat Stanton's long and successful connection with Hibs, but none more so than his being able to trace his family involvement right back to the club's first skipper in 1875. Stanton was brought up in the Craigmillar area of Edinburgh, and came to Hibs via the school side of Holy Cross Academy, and the under-age sides United Crossroads and Salvesens, with whom he won a Lord Weir badge.

He made a scoring debut against Motherwell at inside-left in the autumn of 1963, but soon stepped back, first to wing-half and then, when the new-fangled 4-2-4 formation came into vogue, to sweeper; there he formed a formidable partnership with John McNamee, and then the Dane, John Madsen. There was no better tackler in the country, and Tommy Docherty, no less, stated that Stanton was better than Bobby Moore.

It was in 1966 that he was first capped, against Holland, and appearances at under-23, under-21, league and full international level came along at regular intervals thereafter, and this despite having changed positions again; the arrival of John Blackley meant Hibs had two top-rate sweepers, and Stanton's greater versatility meant that he was the one pushed forward into midfield.

Stanton took over the club captaincy when Joe Davis left Hibs, and was the skipper through the successful period in the early 'seventies, and in particular, two Drybrough Cup wins and the league cup triumph of 1972, in which he scored one goal and made the other.

How that side was broken up by Eddie Turnbull is described earlier. In an effort to provide more strength in what was now a lightweight attack, Stanton was moved further forward. That move failed to inspire a team whose performances and morale were in decline, and though his own form suffered to some extent too, it was an enormous shock when he was transferred to Celtic in 1976, where however no-one grudged him the clutch of medals he earned before what some considered to be a premature retirement after illness in 1978.

It seemed that Stanton's future would be in the game; highly rated as Aberdeen's assistant manager, he then returned to live in Edinburgh, and was successful in running his own show at Cowdenbeath and Dunfermline before

Kenny Waugh brought him back to Easter Road to take over from Bertie Auld in 1982. Unfortunately this brought him little but frustration, from lack of resources to get the team back on the rails, to interference from above, and also what he regarded as clear injustice by the football authorities. Two years was enough, and Stanton resigned in 1984.

Since then, most of his time has been spent in the licensed trade in the east of the city, but Pat is currently involved as an adviser to players on contractal matters. He remains as keen a Hibs' fan as ever, and is a member of the Hibernian Fifty Club.

John Brownlie

AROUND 1950, it is said, Jock Govan moved upfield to join in an attack, and was roundly rebuked by manager Hugh Shaw for his enterprise. That story may be apocryphal, but the change to twenty years later, when John Brownlie's cantripping up the wing was such a thrilling feature of the Scottish game could scarcely be better illustrated.

Brownlie came from the village of Caldercruix, near Airdrie, and was actually a ballboy at Broomfield during his school days. He was invited to play a trial for Aberdeen while Eddie Turnbull was manager there, but his path through the scouting network took him to juvenile football in Edinburgh with Tynecastle Athletic, and then onto the Hibs' ground staff, while he played for Edina Hibs and Pumpherston Juniors.

In those days Brownlie was a central defender, and it was as such that he made his first-team debut against Dunfermline in April 1970. Soon he moved to right-back, where, despite his enthusiasm and aptitude for attacking, he became a regular under Davie Ewing's short spell in charge. Brownlie's flair and confidence were soon noticed further afield, and in June 1971, he played for Scotland against Russia, one of very few Scots teenagers to be capped since the war.

When Eddie Turnbull took over at Easter Road, his attack-conscious team was much more to Brownlie's style, and he revelled in the role, striking up a brilliant partnership with Stanton and Edwards in the right flank of the team which won the 1972 league cup competition, did so well in Europe, and beat Hearts 7-0 on New Year's Day, 1973. Unfortunately, that was the end of what had been a great run, because within a week, Brownlie had broken his leg in a game against East Fife, and it was almost a year before he was able to start a comeback.

By that time, the team as a whole had "peaked", and was in a state of transition, so that Brownlie's role required him to defend more than before. Some viewed this as his failing to recapture his previous fitness and form, but the player disagrees. So did national team boss Willie Ormond, because as early as 1975 he was again invited to play for Scotland.

It was in 1977 that Brownlie followed team-mate John Blackley to Newcastle United, before shorter stays at Middlesbrough, Hartlepool United, Berwick Rangers and Blyth Spartans, followed by managerial experience at Ashington, while he built a career in the financial services sector. In 1989, her returned north of the border, and joined John Blackley at Cowdenbeath.

Alan Rough

"**W**ANTED – ONE GOALKEEPER. Must be able to keep Hibs in the Premier League single-handedly. Apply Easter Road." That was an advert taken from a Hearts' fanzine, and while not intended as a tribute to the big keeper, was exactly that. Alan Rough and Bertie Auld had contrived between them to keep Partick Thistle in the Premier League through the 'seventies, and they were responsible for doing the same job for Hibs at different times in the 'eighties.

Roughie was born in Glasgow, and joined Partick Thistle, where Sammy Kean was the trainer, first on schoolboy forms and then as a professional in 1969. Thistle players do not typically win many honours, but Rough picked up a league cup winner's medal in 1971, and a first division medal in 1976. He had already collected nine under-23 caps, and by the mid-seventies had broken through to the full international side. His save from John Toshack in the 1978 game against Wales at Anfield was one of many unforgettable contributions to the national side, and by 1979 he had overtaken Bill Brown as Scotland's most capped goalkeeper.

More honours followed with Rough being Scottish Player of the Year in 1981 and 1982, but although his name was often linked with Hibs when Bertie Auld was Hibs' boss, it was Pat Stanton who brought him to Easter Road in November 1982 for a £60,000 fee. He was an instant success, immensely popular with the Easter Road support, particularly for his calmness in moments of crisis, and nothing exemplified that more than during another world cup match against Wales, at Cardiff in 1986 when Jim Leighton lost his contact lens and Roughie was called in to take over at half-time.

Rough remained five years at Easter Road, anchoring the team as a succession of managers tried to put Hibs back on the rails, and so his 36th birthday was nigh when Andy Goram was signed. Despite this, Rough's career continued, and he has played for both Celtic and Hamilton Accies at Easter Road. Since then he has joined Ayr United's coaching staff, and has turned out for the Somerset Park team too.

PART FOUR
Matches to Remember

1887
Hibernian 2 – Dumbarton 1

THE FOURTEENTH SCOTTISH CUP FINAL, at Hampden on February 12th, 1887, was Hibs' first big final. They had established themselves as the top team in the east of Scotland by the end of the 'seventies, and had made impressive progress on the national stage during the 'eighties. Their area of recruitment and support had broadened to the point where they had the following of Irish communities throughout Scotland, and they were especially popular in Glasgow.

They had reached the fifth round of the cup in their first essay, and in 1884 were the first east team to reach the semi-finals. Now, after three successive defeats at that stage, they had made the final. It was true that Vale of Leven were not exactly happy about that – they had accused Hibs of paying Willie Groves in breach of the amateur rules; the SFA had arranged the hearing of the protest for the week after the final, and Vale's attempt to get an interdict to prevent the final going ahead had failed.

Dumbartonshire was one of the early hotbeds of Scottish football, with three strong sides in Vale of Leven, Renton and Dumbarton, and it was the last-named, conquerors of Queens Park in the semis, who were Hibs' opponents. The Sons had reached three finals, and had won the cup on one of them.

Hibs arrived at Queen Street Station, we are told, at 2.12 p.m., where they were met by local catholic leaders, and made their way to Hampden for the 3.30 start. About eight thousand spectators seem to have paid, out of over ten thousand in the ground, with an equal number occupying the various vantage points outside the ground, and of them several thousand obtained illegal access during play. Hibs' travelling support, estimated at about a thousand, were distinguished by small green cards on their hats saying "Hurry up Hibs". They had come by train, road, and some had walked – the legendary Dan Fyfe is said to have taken a week for the round trip.

On a pitch slippery after the recent thaw, Hibs applied the early pressure, and Millar headed out from under his bar. The Dumbarton, in blue and white, had the best of it for a while, and claimed a goal, but the ruling was that the ball had passed outside the post – there were no nets in 1887. Fagan headed out from Hibs' goal-line, then Hutcheson did likewise at the other end, as play raged from end to end in a welter of excitement. Towards the interval, Hibs seemed to be gaining the upper hand, with several useful attempts at goal, but had to settle for being level when the whistle blew.

The second half started in much the same way – McGhee had a fine clearance for Hibs; Smith and Clark missed chances at the other end. Then Tobin saved well from Robertson, but when the ball was sent back into the goalmouth, Aitken beat Tobin with a blistering drive.

Hibs retaliated, and Macaulay was charged through his goal just a fraction after parting with the ball. Play died down a little as Dumbarton settled on their lead, but Macaulay made a sorry mess of a shot from Clark from near the corner and it went in, to cheering which lasted for minutes. It was all to play for now, and with only a minute or two to go, Groves made one of his prancing, weaving

Phil Clark.

runs, and passed right to Lafferty who sent the ball past Macaulay while Dumbarton claimed offside. The goal was given, but the wry smile on the face of Hibs' captain McGhee signalled recognition that Hibs, not at their best, had for once had the rub of the green.

Teams:

Hibs – Tobin; Lundy, Fagan; McGhee, McGinn, McLaren; Lafferty, Groves, Montgomery, Clark, Smith.

Dumbarton – Macaulay; Hutcheson, Fergus; Millar McMillan, Kerr; Brown, Robertson, Madden, Aitken, Jamieson.

After the game, the victorious party were entertained to speeches, songs and an excellent supper in St. Mary's School in East Rose Street in the east end of Glasgow before returning by rail to Edinburgh. Their news of course had preceded them, and they were met by two bands and a coach and four, to lead the celebrations at the station, the Tron Kirk and finally St. Mary's Street.

An interesting footnote was the emphasis placed upon the result by Dr. J. Conway M.B., F.R.C.S., who chaired the reception in Glasgow, not only in terms of the self-esteem of Irishmen everywhere, but as lending extra weight to the campaign for home rule for Ireland.

1887
Hibs 2 – Preston North End 1

IN 1887, HIBS, as Scottish Cupholders, and Preston North End, the "Invincibles" from England's professional game, played each other for the "Association Football Championship of the World". At that time there seems little doubt that the winners should be considered to have been the first world club champions.

On the one hand, no major football countries were excluded from consideration, and secondly the competition was taken up by the SFA and the FA, who organised the following year's competition between Renton and West Bromwich Albion at Hampden. That the competition was THEREAFTER discontinued for some time is irrelevant.

The match was the first of its kind, and had been eagerly looked forward to for some time. It was Hibs' first home game of the season, whereas the English side's early season had given Hibs, in any case the underdogs, "scant hopes for success". A little more patience was called for, because the late arrival of Hibs' left winger Clark delayed the kick-off for ten minutes.

When it did get underway, the crowd was treated to a match that was "the hardest fought and, we might say, the roughest that will be witnessed at Easter Road this season".

It started early on; within five minutes it was clear that the "North-Enders had a stiff afternoon's work cut out for them", and almost as soon, "a great deal of feeling was introduced into the game by the rough play of either side". Hibs were determined to give their all and McGhee beat Trainor to give them the lead amid scenes of the wildest enthusiasm.

This put Preston on their mettle, and although Clark and Dunbar combined to miss the half's easiest chance, it was Tobin who had all the difficult saves to keep Hibs ahead to the interval.

Early in the second half, Hibs possessed and won a throw-in near the visitors' posts. A scrimmage ensured, and when it was cleared, it was only as far as McLaren who sent it flying past Trainor for the second goal; the celebrations this time delayed the restart.

As the game progressed, "the superior training" of the professional side appeared to give them the edge, and Hibs, defending defiantly, were pressed back. Gordon hit the post and Dewhurst hit the bar. Clark missed during Hibs' break-out, and Preston at once returned to Tobin's end and Goodall scored with his head.

Play now became very exciting, with the teams equally matched in rough challenges, when suddenly Groves and Smith made a break, the latter centred and McGhee beat Trainor again. A long argument ensued, and much displeasure was displayed when the claim for off-side was upheld, but time was now on Hibs' side. Preston pressed to the call of time, but Hibs held out to be received in tumultuous fashion by their supporters.

Tobin, McLaren, Gallagher, Smith and Groves were singled out for special praise, but all the combatants enjoyed the après-football at the Albert Hotel; Mr Fred Dewhurst warned his hosts that he would demand a day of reckoning for the defeat, and the prospect was warmly relished.

Teams:

Hibs – Tobin; McLaughlin, Lundy; McLaren, McGinn, Gallagher; Smith, Groves, McGhee, Dunbar, Clark.

Preston N. E. – Trainor (Bolton W); Ross, Drummond; Robertson, Ferguson, Weir (Halliwell); Gordon, Ross jun., Goodall, Dewhurst, A. Goodall.

The review of the game noted that it was unlikely that Preston would "have their number taken down again during the course of their present tour" – it was correct, and the tour ended with an 8-1 win over Rangers at Ibrox. Meanwhile, the much-awaited return with Hibs had lost some of its anticipation by the time Hibs travelled to Deepdale and won 4-0 in October 1955.

1902
Hibernian 1 – Celtic 0

HIBS' RECORD IN SCOTTISH CUP FINALS is second to just about everybody's, and so their last success in Scotland's senior competition, in 1902, has a special significance. They had not had a great league season, finishing seventh out of ten, but had beaten Port Glasgow, Queens Park and Clyde in the early rounds of the cup.

Hibs had beaten Rangers in the semi-finals, but at a cost, as their right winger, Willie McCartney, had broken his leg. Semi-finals were still not held at neutral venues, and so Hibs had to travel to Glasgow. Nowadays such a game would be held on neutral ground, and Hibs would have to travel to Glasgow. The final against Celtic, of course, was held on neutral ground. The ground in question was Celtic Park.

This, to be fair, was because Ibrox had recently been the scene of the first fatal accident at Rangers' ground, at an international match against England, and Hampden was being rebuilt, and if nothing else, it provided Hibs with the rare distinction of winning Scottish Cup ties on all of the big Glasgow grounds in the same season.

The preparations for this important occasion were suitably thorough, even if at odds with modern thinking – the players were confined to the ground during the evenings to prevent them taking advantage of the social facilities in the town, while they were plied with mugs of hot chocolate and doormat-style sandwiches.

The crowd was around fifteen thousand, and perhaps the gale-force wind which swept the length of Parkhead had dissuaded some from attending. Those who stayed away certainly missed little in a dull first half; that suited Hibs, who were playing into the gale. Harrower was doing a fine marking job on Sandy McMahon, who had been an Easter Road star in the latter days of the "old" Hibs, and with Celtic unable to harness the wind, Rennie had a fairly comfortable passage.

In the second half, the gale had increased a notch or two on the Beaufort scale, to the point where clearances from the Celtic defence were being blown back into the goalmouth, or for corners. There seemed little chance of Celtic making the hundred odd yards necessary to threaten Rennie's charge, but suddenly Livingstone broke away, and his shot beat Rennie and came back off the woodwork, where McCafferty, following up, made a mess of the rebound.

A breakthrough at Celtic's end seemed imminent, and Atherton seemed to have got it with a splendid goal which he was dismayed to find disallowed, but the lead was not long delayed. Paddy Callaghan took a corner, and Andy McGeechan wheeled to shoot into the net; the story persists that he did a fine imitation of the Celtic goalkeeper's distinctive brogue to persuade full back Battles to leave the ball as it came across. Celtic protested, but as the referee had heard nothing wrong, it was appropriate for him to turn a deaf ear. That livened things up; every Hibs attack now bore menace, while the Parkhead defence showed signs of wilting. As so often happens when the onslaught bore no fruit, a last-minute counter attack almost brought an equaliser for Celtic.

Teams:

Hibs – Rennie; Gray, Glen; Breslin, Harrower, Robertson; McCall, McGeachan, Divers, Callaghan, Atherton.

Celtic – McFarlane; Watson, Battles; Lonie, Marshall, Orr; McCafferty, McDermott, McMahon, Livingstone, Quinn.

Referee – Mr. Murray (Stenhousemuir).

The cup was presented to Hibs' club president, Mr. Philip Farmer, in the Alexandra Hotel, there was a band to see Hibs off at Queen Street, and there was another to meet them at Haymarket. A brake carried the team, with captain Bobby Atherton holding aloft the trophy, along Princes Street to the Waverley Station, where traffic had been stopped because of a reception by a crowd of ten thousand – the biggest welcome yet for a cupwinning side – and it was the sixth time in sixteen years that the trophy had come to the capital.

1941
Hibernian 8 – Rangers 1

RANGERS FOOTBALL CLUB, often wrongly called Glasgow Rangers, is a proud club. In July 1941, they lost the Summer Cup final to Hibs after leading by two goals. That did not happen very often to Rangers teams of these times, and their pride was hurt. When they came to Easter Road on league business in the last week of September, bristling with internationalists and indignation, they were bent on revenge.

The Hibs team could not boast the same experience – only "Li'l Arthur" Milne and the recently signed Jimmy Caskey from Everton had any to speak of, and at the other end of the scale, Gordon Smith and Bobby Combe were just seventeen. But as with most wartime line-ups, there was a generous lacing of guests, and Hibs fielded four.

Bobby Baxter, Middlesbrough's international centre-half, captained Hibs. Joe Crozier from Brentford was another Scottish cap, and deputised for Jimmy Kerr in goal. Bob Hardisty, an amateur cap then of Wolves and later Bishop Auckland, used to infuriate Baxter by his enthusiastic chasing of the ball all over the park, and finally Alex Hall was a full back from Sunderland, and something of a ringer for backs of the time – small, tigerish, hair combed straight back and a line in tackling which would make Graeme Souness look dainty.

Rangers had opened up a four point gap at the top after only seven games, but Hibs were expected to give them the toughest test so far. The quota limit of fifteen thousand was inside Easter Road long before the kick-off, having paid the improbable amount of thirteen pence for the privilege.

There was little doubt that Hibs already deserved the lead they got as early as the seventh minute. Caskie sallied down the left, Combe headed the cross in the right direction, and Milne hooked it into the net. Milne got through again but shot past under pressure, Finnegan had a rocket of a shot blocked by Dawson, and the crowd, now certainly far in excess of the official limit, warmed to Rangers getting a going over.

They enjoyed the 22nd minute too, with Combe volleying home Hibs' second, before there was a slight hiccup – a clumsy run by Rangers' Smith was halted by Baxter, and to the general surprise, the referee gave a penalty. Venters made it 2-1, but before the interval, Gordon Smith raced in to get his head to a Caskie corner and restored the two-goal lead.

Rangers were not taking their discomfiture very well, and Gillick for one was spoken to, and for a while after the interval, the tiny Hibs' attack were finding their lack of weight a disadvantage. Smith conceded two fouls and had his name taken. But just as Rangers might have been thinking that this was their route back, Milne blasted a fourth goal from a glorious cross from Caskie, and within a minute, Combe had left Dawson helpless from thirty yards; Hibs were home and dry with half an hour left.

But the excitement was not over. Twice in a minute, Combe tricked a couple of defenders and beat Dawson with fine drives, and with three minutes to go, Smith made it eight. Milne got through yet again, going for his hat-trick. He rounded Dawson only to miss as only he could, and the goalkeeper asked him "Have you stopped trying now, Arthur?"

To add to Rangers' misery, Venters was sent off near the end for a loss of temper.

Teams:

Hibs – Crozier; Shaw, Hall; Hardisty, Baxter, Kean; Smith, Finnegan, Milne, Combe, Caskie.

Rangers – Dawson; Gray, Shaw; Bolt, Woodburn, Little; McIntosh, Gillick, Smith, Venters, Johnstone.

Referee – M. C. Hutton (Glasgow).

The return match took place around Christmas. An understrength Hibs side went to Ibrox and could muster only one attack – but it ended with Bobby Combe scoring the game's only goal.

1951
Rangers 2 – Hibernian 3

TWO OF THE FEATURES of the Famous Five era in the early 'fifties were, firstly, the clashes between that quintet and the so-called Rangers "iron curtain", and, secondly, the high scoring which came about when the mood took them. One of the classic encounters between Hibs and Rangers was the Scottish Cup second-round tie at Ibrox in February 1951; Rangers' cup record in recent times had certainly been better than Hibs' – they had won the trophy for the previous three years.

The gates were closed with more than one hundred and two thousand spectators in the ground, and many others in the car park, congregated in knots around the few buses equipped with wireless.

The Scotsman described the game as the perfect cup-tie, and the excitement was at fever-pitch from start to finish. There was not a lot of room, but the Rangers fans made the most of what there was when Simpson scored in just four minutes. There was a suggestion of good fortune in the execution of it, but it was nevertheless a severe blow to Hibs, and for a while they were hard put to avoid further disaster. But gradually the storm was weathered, and Hibs started to put together some moves of their own, and swing play towards Brown. With five minutes to the interval, they had their reward when Gordon Smith fired a Willie Ormond cross into the net to equalise.

Having come back so well, Hibs were a happier bunch at the break, but the feeling did not persist; just two minutes after resuming, they were back where they started. A neat bout of interpassing involved several Ibrox players and Simpson neatly finished it off. This time Rangers fell back into defence, not a widely used tactic in these attack-conscious days, but one which had served the Ibrox side well on occasion.

Consequently the second half developed into the battle between Hibs' forwards and the Rangers' defence which most expected to have been the case anyway. Hibs' halfbacks were generally free to join their forwards in the assault, and after twenty-five minutes, Eddie Turnbull brought them level with what was surely the hardest twenty-yarder he had ever hit. Rangers were unable to respond in attack, and five minutes later, another of their defensive ploys resulted in a free kick for Hibs not far outside the penalty area.

The situation seemed ideal for another Turnbull rocket, but the inside left passed short to Bobby Johnstone instead, and he, spotting Brown marginally off his line, spooned the ball over the wall and the goalkeeper into the top corner of

Gordon Smith scores the equaliser.

the net. Johnstone's exhuberant expression of his delight at his own genius earned him some criticism at the time, although in today's world it would seem extremely restrained.

Teams:

Rangers – Brown; Young, Shaw; McColl, Woodburn, Cox; Waddell, Thomson, Simpson, Rae, Paterson.

Hibernian – Younger; Govan, Ogilvie; Buchanan, Paterson, Gallagher; Smith, Johnstone, Reilly, Turnbull, Ormond.

To most sides, meeting Rangers at Ibrox would have posed the biggest problem in their quest for cup success, but with Hibs it was otherwise, and their Tynecastle bogey struck again with a vengeance. Hibs reached the semi-finals and were drawn to play Motherwell in Gorgie, but lost Ogilvie with a broken leg and Ormond with ruptured ligaments on their way to a 3-2 defeat.

1952
Hibs 7 – Manchester United 3

GORDON SMITH signed for Hibs in 1941, and played his five hundredth game for the club in August 1952. The occasion was the opening league cup-tie of the season against Queen of the South, but instead of it being a gala occasion for the Hibs' skipper, it turned out to be a personal triumph for Johnstone – not the perky little Hibs' inside man, but the balding toothless veteran winger who embarrassingly upstaged the whole Hibs' forward line and inspired the Doonhamers to a 3-1 win.

To mark the five hundredth game landmark, Smith was given a testimonial, with Matt Busby's Manchester United the guests on September 15th. By then Hibs had found some form, won their league cup section, and, just two days before the United game, the Famous Five had shown what they were famous for by winning 6-0 against Morton at Greenock. Hibs also had a record against English opposition which was second to none, and the large crowd relished the prospect of another notable scalp.

They also saw a feast of football which drew superlatives from all quarters. *The Scotsman's* representative considered it to be the finest exhibition of football artistry he had witnessed, and certainly there was more in common with the Real Madrid-Eintracht Frankfurt game of 1960 than the score.

It took fifteen minutes for the first goal to come; Smith went down the right, and aimed a cross for Ormond on the other flank; McNulty got his head to the ball to prevent this, but his header out fell for Turnbull to crash the ball into the net off the unlucky McNulty. United, however, has their own long-range expert in Rowley, and seven minutes later, he beat McCracken all ends up from outside the area. Rowley was causing all kinds of bother, and he beat the young Hibs' keeper again on the half hour with a deceptively spinning shot.

Hibs took up the challenge, and some furious attacking brought reward with a penalty kick for hands against Chiltern. Turnbull's effort was blocked, but he crashed the rebound home. That was in 42 minutes, but before the break, Pearson sent in a shot which McCracken saw late, and the ball went under his body to give United an interval lead.

The second half saw one of Hibs' great fightbacks as they tore the English champions apart, and quite apart from the plethora of goals, there was no let-up in the action. Devine's shot hit the bar, Reilly had a goal disallowed and Gallacher made an ungainly goal-line clearance before Ormond equalised in 62 minutes amid frantic excitement. McNulty had a second "assist" for Hibs by fouling

Reilly, and Turnbull blasted home the penalty, and then Rowley was denied his hat-trick by an acrobatic goal-line clearance by Paterson. United were next denied a goal because of offside, and Carey missed from the penalty spot, to leave the score at 4-3.

Smith contributed to his cause with a goal from a rebound from the United goalkeeper; Reilly eventually got onto the scoresheet by heading home a cross by Smith, just after a white ball had been brought on, and in the gathering darkness, Turnbull hit a terrific left-foot drive high into the net.

Teams:

Hibs – McCracken; Govan, Howie; Gallacher, Paterson, Combe; Smith, Johnstone, Reilly, Turnbull, Ormond.

Manchester United – Wood; McNulty, Aston; Carey, Chiltern, Gibson; Scott, Downie, Rowley, Pearson, Berry.

Referee – J. A. Mowat (Rutherglen).

That was not the end of the high scoring – just two days later came another six, against Morton in the second leg of the league cup tie, and on the following Saturday, Reilly scored a hat-trick against Hearts, to bring Hibs' tally to twenty-two in a week.

1961
Hibernian 3 – Barcelona 2

REAL MADRID won the first five European Cup competitions, culminating in their famous win over Eintracht Frankfurt at Hampden in 1960. They were not champions of Spain, however. Barcelona had won the Spanish double in 1959, and retained the league title in 1960. They had beaten AC Milan (7-1) and English champions Wolves (9-2) before losing to Real in the 1960 European Cup semi-finals, and were holders of the Fairs Cup (the forerunner to the UEFA Cup).

In 1960-61, Barcelona were in both competitions again, and reaffirmed their domestic superiority on the international stage by eliminating Real from the Champions' Cup in the second round, to become undisputed top dogs in Europe. In the Fairs Cup, they were paired with Hibs. It remains a pity that the trouble which concluded the tie between the two should be allowed to detract from the greatest result that any Scottish side has ever achieved in European competition.

Hibs meanwhile were in a state of transition, and recovering from a terrible start to the season – they were to finish eighth in the table come April. It was probably to Hibs' advantage, then, that fog caused the first leg in Edinburgh to be cancelled, and they flew out to the Mediterranean at Christmas time. Few gave them any chance, but Hibs led 2-0, and then 4-2 with six minutes left, before having to settle for a 4-4 draw. Back home they were credited with a giant fluke.

By the time that Barcelona returned to Scotland in February, some of the polish seemed to have deserted their domestic form, Stewart Brown forecast a narrow win for Hibs, and over 50,000 fans packed Easter Road to see if he was right. And in ten minutes they were dancing. Johnny Macleod clipped a free kick goalwards, and Joe Baker rose in front of Medrano to flick the ball into the net.

There were signs of panic every time the speedy and aggressive centre had possession, but as minutes passed without further disaster, the Spaniards put their moves together with increasing menace, and on the half-hour Martinez silenced the crowd by wheeling to shoot home from close range. Worse followed for Hibs when the Hungarian Koscis controlled a ball that seemed to be going behind him and stroked it past Ronnie Simpson to make it 2-1 at half-time.

The passion and commitment of Hibs' second-half surge down the slope could not have been excelled, against a rearguard which was under even more strain to hold the line.

In twenty minutes, Baker was spreadeagled in the box and little consoled by an indirect free kick; the tackles rose with the tension, until with fifteen minutes left, the stadium erupted. Willie Ormond, in his final season with Hibs, took a corner, Sammy Baird headed goalwards and Tommy Preston reached it before Medrano to head home.

The pressure continued, and ten minutes later Macleod was brought down in full flight by Garay, Herr Malka pointed to the spot and was immediately assailed by the Spaniards. It was some minutes before the kick could be taken, and with the pressure even getting to the experienced Sammy Baird, Bobby Kinloch realised that his one chance of footballing immorality had come, and stepped up to beat Medrano. Immediately, Medrano, Suarez and others made for the referee again, and the official was on the ground by the time the police arrived to rescue him. It seemed incredible that, far from being arrested, not one player was cautioned, and play continued after several minutes.

The remaining five minutes lasted ten and seemed like twenty, before Herr Malka blew the whistle and was immediately engulfed by waiting policemen. Thus everyone went home happy, except of course the Spaniards, and Harry Swan, who had already sold the home rights for the third game.

Teams:

Hibernian – Simpson; Fraser, McLelland; Baxter, Easton, Baird; Macleod, Preston, Baker, Kinloch, Ormond.

Barcelona – Medrano; Foncho, Garay; Verges, Gensana, Segarra; Evaristo, Koscis, Martinez, Suarez, Villaverde.

Referee – J. Malka (West Germany).

1964
Hibernian 2 – Real Madrid 0

SOMEONE ONCE ASKED PAT STANTON who the best player he ever played with, or against, was, and Stanton's answer was Willie Hamilton; Jock Stein, who overheard the conversation, did not disagree. Praise indeed, and there was no more virtuoso display by the fair-haired inside man than the night when he inspired Hibs to lower Real Madrid's colours in Scotland for the first time.

The date was October 7th, 1964; Jock Stein was manager at Easter Road. He had taken over at the tail end of the previous season, and had guided Hibs to their Summer Cup win just a month earlier. Hibs had played in the Fairs Cup the three previous seasons with some success despite their domestic problems, and had acquired the habit. With no involvement this time round, Stein, thinking big as always, brought the famous Spanish team to Easter Road for a challenge match. Real did not play "frendlies" as such in these days, and neither did Stein.

Their initiative cost Hibs a hefty guarantee, and prices had to be increased to pay for it – the terracing cost 6/-, or 30p nowadays, and even then the attendance of thirty thousand was not quite enough for Hibs to break even. Maybe some had been discouraged by W.H. Kemp, forecasting a non-event and seven goals for Real in *The Scotsman*.

There was an air of mystery about the Hibs line-up; even Stein had failed thus far to blend two similar ball-players as Willie Hamilton and Pat Quinn into the same team, and the diminutive ex-Motherwell man had been out of the side and unhappy with his lot. Against Real, Stein promised, both would play. There was plenty of competition for places – Hibs had Eric Stevenson and Jimmy O'Rourke on the bench. If Real were past their magical best, they still had players like Puskas, Gento and Amancio in their side.

Real started in a slow arrogant manner, Gento's rocket shot was deflected by Hibs' captain John Fraser, and a curling effort by Puskas had Wilson scrambling at the post, but with the Hibs halfbacks giving the Spaniards less and less space, this phase did not last long. Quinn was operating very deep, Hamilton up front, and the supply to the front-runners soon got underway. In the thirteenth minute it produced sensational results – Hamilton fed Neil Martin out on the left, and Martin's knee-high cross was met on the volley by Peter Cormack and the ball was low past Araquistain in a flash.

Real were stunned, and they did not find it easy to hit back. While Hamilton was lord of midfield, Puskas was well and truly shackled by Stanton and Baxter, while Fraser was having the game of his life against Gento. For a spell, Real seemed content to hold the ball and bide their time, but once the second half was underway, there appeared a new sense of urgency.

This was the real test for Hibs. Each time Real tried to increase the tempo, Hibs responded, and as the half wore on, they were getting no nearer Wilson, and some desperation crept into their play. With soaring confidence, Hibs applied pressure of their own, and met some unsubtle defending, and then suddenly, it was all over – Quinn took a free-kick on the right, and Hamilton dummied it so that the unlucky Zoco glanced it past his keeper into the net. There were only six minutes to go, and the celebrations of a famous victory had begun.

Stewart Brown was able to divulge, as a measure of that achievement, that, outwith their domestic commitments, Real had only failed to score on four occasions since the European Cup started in 1955, and had drawn all four away from home, and meanwhile, his colleague Mr. Kemp had been escorted by Mr. Stein to the Hibs' dressing room to meet the players he had so underrated.

Teams:

Hibs – Wilson; Fraser, Parke; Stanton, McNamee, Baxter; Cormack, Hamilton, Scott, Quinn, Martin.

Real Madrid – Araquistain; Miera, Pachin; Muller, Santamaria, Zoco, Amancio, Ruiz, Grosso, Puskas, Gento.

Referee – Hugh Phillips (Wishaw).

Hibs went from Real to Ibrox on the Saturday, and the well-known pre-match discussion between Hamilton and Jim Baxter about which of them was going to show the other up. Pleasing to report, Hamilton was again in magical form, and Hibs won 4-2.

1967
Hibernian 5 – Naples 0

THINGS HAD NOT GONE TOO WELL FOR HIBS IN ITALY; while not actually dying as a result of seeing Naples, they seemed to have come to the end of their run in the 1967-68 Fairs Cup. Things were not going too well for the country as a whole either, because while Hibs were abroad, sterling was devalued by about fourteen per cent, and they were unable to pay their hotel bill!

Colin Stein had scored an away goal for Hibs, but the Italians had scored four. The system of away goals was still something of a novelty, and the Hibs' programme featured yet another explanation for those who were still baffled. Few thought that it would come to away goals in any case – Naples were the domestic league leaders, and Italian football was still to emerge from the Herrera era of catenaccio, so that the prospect of Hibs scoring three goals seemed remote.

The date was 29th November 1967, and, although there was hardly a Hibs' fan of the time who does not claim to have been present, the ground was less than half full, with 21,037 spectators inside.

It was not long before the action started; within five minutes, full-back Bobby Duncan picked up a loose ball in his own half, and strode forward with it

Pat Stanton scores Hibs' fourth goal.

before unleashing a shot from far outside the penalty area which caught Zoff slightly off his line and his guard, and the ball flashed wide of the goalkeeper and high into the net. It was Duncan's first goal for the club.

Almost at once, Cormack was brought down inside the box, and an indirect free kick brought scant justice, and then the game settled into a pattern; Naples had come to defend, and with a packed penalty area in front of an excellent goalkeeper, chances were few despite a constant bombardment by the Hibs attack driven on by Stanton. At the other end, Naples, missing Altafini, were being easily contained by Madsen and his backs, allowing the Hibs' midfield to join the assault on goal. Zoff had a brilliant save from Stanton's header, and Blanchi cleared an overhead kick from Stein off the line, but the defence held firm. That was until the crucial minute before half-time – Stein was fouled yet again, but got in a shot; the ball rebounded to Quinn and he calmly stroked it into the corner of the net.

The Italians were shaken, and they sent on another defender, Girardo, in the second half to hold what remained of their lead. It didn't reduce the rate of free-kicks – rather the reverse as the pressure was stepped up down the slope – but it introduced a new angle as the substitute and Blanchi were cautioned for impeding the taking of them. The Italian defence was by now looking far from secure, and Orlando lost the place and threw a punch before the inevitable breakthrough came in 67 minutes.

Alex Scott took a corner on the right, and Peter Cormack rose spring-heeled to head home strongly at the near post. The atmosphere was terrific now, with the crowd largely crammed into the bottom end of the ground, and while the celebrations were still in full swing Scott got possession again on the right, and this time delivered the perfect far-post cross for Stanton to score with a low header.

By now Naples were demoralised, and their case was not helped by the continuing indiscretion of Girardo, who was sent off for kicking Stevenson. The Italians did make efforts to attack which, with so many defenders in the team, was pretty ineffectual, whereas Hibs, tails up, were now finding even more space, and looked likely to score again. With eleven minutes to go they did; Eric Stevenson got away on the left, and Stein ran on to his cross to blast the ball delicately past Zoff's ear to make it five. Possibly the greatest of Hibs' many notable fightbacks down their slope was now complete.

Teams:

Hibs – Wilson; Duncan, Davis; Stanton, Madsen, McGraw; Scott, Quinn, Stein, Cormack, Stevenson. Subs – Simpson, O'Rourke, McNeil.

Napoli – Zoff; Nardin, Pegliaro; Zurlini, Panzanato, Blanchi; Cane, Juliano, Orlando, Montefusco, Barisen. Subs – Girardo, Cuman, Bosdaves.

Referee – A. Rigo (Spain).

1972
Hibs 6 – Sporting Lisbon 1

THIS WAS THE FIRST TIE that Hibs had ever played in the European Cupwinners' Cup. It was more a reward for reaching the final of the 1972 Scottish Cup than for what happened when they got there.

The first leg was in Portugal in mid-September; Hibs surprised Sporting in two ways – the first was their brand new purple strip, and the second their willingness to have a go. Cropley hit a post in the first minute, but no goals came. Then Sporting scored twice in two minutes in the second half, and it took an Arthur Duncan goal to give Hibs a good 1-2 away result.

Press comments from Hibs' players suggested no lack of confidence, but the first half at Easter Road did little to justify it. It was something of a struggle, especially in the midfield where the dominance and style of Fraguito caused a great deal of frustration for Stanton, Cropley and O'Rourke. In fact, O'Rourke recalls collecting the ball to take a throw-in near the end of this period and being invited by a well-wisher to help his team by leaving the pitch!

Still, Hibs did take the lead in 28 minutes, a typical Gordon header from an Edwards cross, and the 26,000 crowd celebrated being in front, albeit only on away goals. It lasted only a few minutes, until Marinho took a lucky deflection off the referee, and his cross was smashed home by Yazaldi.

The second half was a different story, with Hibs kicking down the hill, and Edwards and Duncan causing trouble on both flanks. Duncan had one run which looked like yielding the goal of the season, Damas twice saved well, but in ten minutes, Hibs scored – Gordon flicked the ball goalwards, and O'Rourke coolly lobbed the stranded goalkeeper.

Two minutes later, John Brownlie lashed a shot against the post, and two minutes after that Gordon headed another goal from a Schaedler cross. The Portuguese defence was crumbling fast now, and in 63 minutes O'Rourke scored from a Brownlie pass.

Sporting used both substitutes to stem the flow, but it was too late. O'Rourke completed his hat-trick from the penalty spot when the flying Duncan was upended, and then when Duncan was through again and should have scored himself, Manaca turned his misdirected cross into the net to complete Sporting Lisbon's worst defeat in European football.

Ronnie Allen, Sporting's English manager, charitably suggested that his goalkeeper had given away four of the goals, but all that concerned Hibs was the second-round draw.

Teams:

Hibs – Herriot; Brownlie, Schaedler; Stanton, Black, Blackley; Edwards, O'Rourke, Gordon, Cropley, Duncan.

Sporting Lisbon – Damas; Gomez, Pereira; Chiro (Dinis), Manaca, Laranjeiro; Marinho, Fraquito, Yazaldi, Nelson, Wagner (Tome).

Referee – G. Maening (DDR).

1972
Hibernian 2 – Celtic 1

GIVEN HIBS' RECORD of cup final disasters since their last Scottish Cup win in 1902, their successful venture in the 1972 League Cup is an inescapable inclusion in any tally of memorable Hibernian occasions. In the context of the time, it was also important for establishing their position amongst the front runners of the Scottish game – in the second half of 1972, these amounted to only Hibs and Celtic.

Hibs had recovered from one or two drubbings by the Parkhead side in the previous few years, and not least the 6-1 defeat in the 1972 Scottish Cup final – by winning the Drybrough Cup in the summer, overcoming a pitch invasion when they were three up and Celtic's subsequent fight back to equality, to do it. They had also beaten Rangers in the semi-finals of three cups during the year, to remove the Ibrox side from the role of credible alternative champions, but the feeling was that they had still to prove themselves on the big occasion, and especially against Jock Stein's men, and take on that mantle, themselves.

Rivals for by no means the first time, managers Stein and Turnbull each had a tactical ploy in mind; Arthur Duncan was to play on the right, presumably

because his pace was expected to trouble Brogan, while Jimmy Johnstone was set to perform on the left, perhaps to keep Brownlie's attention away from his love of attack. If Duncan failed to provide a first-half breakthrough for Hibs, then Johnstone had a worse time of it – Brownlie first gathered points by reading a backheeler from the tiny redhead, and then started one of the very runs which Johnstone was supposed to prevent, by bouncing the ball off the shins of the one-time terror of Europe. Johnstone's contribution to the game was effectively over, and he was later substituted. The opening half therefore became something of a midfield struggle, but Hibs survived Celtic's burst of attack before the break, and would have been the happier lot with the half-time score 0-0.

The second half was a different matter: Turnbull sent Duncan to the left wing, with Edwards operating between outside right, and the middle of the field. The Hibs attack looked better balanced, and they scored on the hour. McNeill fouled Gordon outside the penalty area, and when Edwards floated the free kick just over the "wall" to Stanton, the Hibs' skipper veered away from goal, seeming to have missed his chance, only to turn and slot the ball past Williams. This was the break Hibs needed, confidence soared, and for ten minutes they put Celtic through the mill. Edwards found Stanton running wide on the right, Stanton took the ball without breaking stride, and, with Alan Gordon waiting on the far post, picked out instead Jimmy O'Rourke haring in on the near one, and O'Rourke's header flashed past Williams. Next, McNeill knew little about a Gordon shot which struck him on the line with his keeper stranded, and a minute after that, Stanton strode through the middle again, and sent a shot against Williams' right-hand post.

The large Hibs support were enjoying the mayhem which they had seen in reverse more than once, but they also had to get through what seemed an eternity of nailbiting – there were still fifteen minutes on the clock when a fine forward pass from Connolly just beat Schaedler to leave Kenny Dalglish to run in on McArthur and halve the deficit. It would have been an injustice if Celtic had pulled the game out of the fire, and, as always, they spared no effort in trying to do so, but ultimately Mr. McKenzie blew his whistle, and Pat Stanton became the first Hibs' skipper for seventy years to hold aloft a major trophy.

Teams:

Hibs – Herriot; Brownlie, Schaedler; Stanton, Black, Blackley; Edwards, O'Rourke, Gordon, Cropley, Duncan. Sub – Hamilton.

Celtic – Williams; McGrain, Connolly; McCluskey, McNeill, Hay; Johnstone, Connolly, Dalglish, Hood, Macari. Sub – Callaghan.

Referee – Mr. A. McKenzie (Larbert).

1973
Hearts 0 – Hibernian 7

THE FIRST DAY OF JANUARY 1973 was a historic one; Britain at last entered the European Economic Community. It was also the hundredth league derby between Hearts and Hibs since automatic promotion and relegation, and, as the match programme pointed out, Hearts were one up in the series. It was also Donald Ford's 300th game for Hearts, and if Donald had yet to break his scoring duck against Hibs, then no other Hearts player had scored a league goal against Hibs since 1968 either.

It is often forgotten that Hearts were having a good season, and had been third in the table until the last couple of games. Hibs on the other hand had swept through to win the league cup and reach the European Cupwinners' Cup quarter-finals. They were also challenging for the league, lying just two points behind Celtic, and they were scoring a lot of goals.

For a few minutes, there were signs of a competitive game, and one near thing when Donald Park shot wide from a good position. The Hibs settled down, and everything started happening for them. Before they scored, they seemed to be completely in control of the middle of the field, and Arthur Duncan's pace had already sent panic signals flying in the Tynecastle defence – and they scored in nine minutes.

Erich Schaedler launched one of his long throws from the left, Thomson

Alan Gordon scores the seventh goal.

misread the bounce completely so the ball bounced over his head, and O'Rourke cracked it high into the net from close range. Six minutes later, Alex Edwards picked out Alan Gordon with a long ball to the edge of the penalty area; Gordon took it on the chest, slipped in turning, but calmly hooked the ball past Garland nevertheless. In twenty-five minutes, Cropley intercepted a clearance, and his header found the defence caught square and in no position to catch Duncan as he raced in on goal to beat Garland again. Late arriving Hibs fans were now meeting Hearts supporters on their way home.

In thirty-five minutes, Cropley made it four with a thrilling volley from just outside the box, and two minutes later, Duncan headed a fifth off a post from another Edwards cross. It was 5-0 at half-time, and might have been more. Edwards in particular was toying with the defence, and looked certain to score from four yards when he lost concentration. When Edwards caught the Hearts wall cold by spooning a free kick over it, O'Rourke hooked a volley just past.

It had been a mesmerising performance, and inevitably the second half was less so; Hibs were content to play with the ball, but looked dangerous whenever they took on the Hearts defence. With Celtic idle, they had to score six to take over the league leadership, and it took just another ten minutes to get there. Stanton picked up a pass in midfield and drove right through the defence to force Garland to leave his goal to meet him. Stanton's measured shot would have found the net on its own, but the ever alert O'Rourke arrived to make sure from a yard or so out. The rout was completed with fifteen minutes left. Schaedler lost possession by putting the ball too far ahead, but was still able to force it through to Duncan, whose high cross was headed past Garland by Alan Gordon off the far post in exemplary fashion. The final whistle gave the feeling of waking up from a dream.

Teams:

Hearts – Garland; Clunie, Jeffries; Thomson, Anderson, Wood; Park, Brown, Ford, Carruthers, Murray. Sub – Lynch.

Hibs – Herriot; Brownlie, Schaedler; Stanton, Black, Blackley; Edwards, O'Rourke, Gordon, Cropley, Duncan. Sub – Hamilton.

The referee was J.P.R. Gordon of Newport, a late stand-in for Bill Mullan, who was indisposed following a car accident.

That afternoon proved to be the culmination of the achievements of that Hibs team; with Edwards and Brownlie out for long spells, they never recaptured the same magic. The effect on Hearts was more traumatic – they managed only two more goals at Tynecastle during the remainder of the season, and when Hibs returned there in September, they had still more league goals at Tynecastle to their credit than their hosts.

1989
Videoton 0 – Hibernian 3

HIBS' EUROPEAN VENTURE OF 1989-90 was their first for over a decade, and a new experience for a generation of players and supporters to whom Reims, Barcelona and Naples were just names. Those who made the long trip to Hungary were rewarded with a result of which any of Hibs' previous European teams would have been proud.

Even although the iron curtain was beginning to crack, it seemed a daunting trip behind it. Videoton had reached the UEFA Cup final just four years earlier, and had held Real Madrid to a 3-1 aggregate. At Easter Road, feeling in no way threatened by the weakest of referees, their physical tactics had held Hibs to a single goal, scored by Graham Mitchell with a looping header when Sneddon quickly returned a ball which the goalkeeper had punched out.

A large and noisy support had followed Hibs to Szekesfehervar, and they brought a carnival atmosphere which seemed somewhat foreign to the drab Hungarian town thirty miles from Budapest. The introduction of the star prize in a local competition improved their humour further – it was a Lada.

When the game got under way before a crowd of 16,166 spectators, it was clear that Hibs were not there to defend their small lead. Mitchell had evidently been singled out by the opposition, and he had been targeted even before the ninth minute. when he rode a heavy tackle on the edge of the penalty area and crossed perfectly for Keith Houchen to steer a header past Petry into the net.

This gave Hibs the cushion they wanted, and their play oozed confidence. The Hungarians had less say in what happened to the ball, partly because they were paying increasing attention to their opponents instead. Mitchell was injured in another incident with Takacz, so that he was unable to resume after the interval, and Collins was involved in a flare-up with the same player after another bad tackle.

Pat McGinlay replaced Mitchell at half-time, and on resumption, the Hungarian escalated their assaults to the point where the referee, who had done a good job in control to that point, had to take further action. An off-the-ball assault by Sprecksak went unnoticed but the next one by Petras on Neil Cooper was spotted by a linesman, and the perpetrator was swiftly sent off.

Kuttor was booked for a foul on Sneddon, the home supporters followed up with a barrage of missiles, and it seemed as though the home team had completely lost the place. A minute later they had certainly lost the match too; Houchen, the best player on view, struck the post with a header from Sneddon's free kick and Gareth Evans rammed home the rebound.

This drew the sting from Videoton. The remaining half-hour was played out at exhibition pace, and the Hibs fans sang happily about goulash. A third goal capped a fine display; with eleven minutes to go Brian Hamilton struck the bar with a vicious thirty-yarder, the ball broke to John Collins on the left, and his shot on the volley rasped into the net. All that remained to think about was a long trip home.

Teams:

Videoton – Petry, Koszata, Horvath, Laszlo, Kuttor, Takacz, Jonas, Manasi, Quiriko, Csucsansky, Petres. Subs – Nemeth, Babai, Spreksak, Tintar, Muller.

Hibs – Goram, Kane, Sneddon, Cooper, Mitchell, Hunter, Hamilton, Orr, Houchen, Collins, Evans. Subs – Reid, Milne, Weir, McGinlay, Archibald.

Referee – K.J. Assenmacher (BRD).

PART FIVE

Hibs Today

Andy Goram (Club captain)

Son of Lew Goram, also a goalkeeper who was on Hibs' books in the post-war era, Andy was born in Bury in Lancashire. He was an apprentice at West Bromwich, but signed for Hibs from Oldham Athletic for a club record fee of £325,000 in October 1987. Andy was noticed first by English selectors, but chose Scotland, and was already an under-21 and full cap before joining Hibs. He won a further clutch of caps last season, and was unlucky not to get his game in Italy during the summer. Now 26, he has matured into the best goalkeeper in the country. Shares with Scot Symon the distinction of having represented Scotland at football and cricket.

Neil Cooper

£40,000 is a bargain price for a player in the Premier League, and that is exactly what Hibs got in signing the experienced Neil Cooper from St. Mirren in 1989. It was Alex Miller who had taken Neil to Paisley six years earlier, after previous stops at Aberdeen, Barnsley and Grimsby Town. Neil has schoolboy and youth caps to his credit, as well as a Scottish Cupwinners' medal; an Aberdonian, he celebrated his thirty-second birthday during the summer break, and brings experience and authority to Hibs' defence.

David Fellinger

A local lad, David signed for Hibs in 1985 from Hutchison Vale, the same club as John Collins came from, and displays some of the same characteristics as his illustrious predecessor, such as strength in the tackle and courage for one so small. Capped by Scotland as a schoolboy, David has played a number of first-team games, and opened his goals tally against Dundee United last season.

Billy Findlay

Born in Kilmarnock and signed from Kilmarnock Boys Club in 1987, Billy left his teenage years behind him in the close season. He has made a handful of appearances in the Premier League, and opened his goalscoring account in the last game of 1988-89 against Dundee. Billy required only some extra muscle to add to his obvious skills to be a success in the first team, when Hibs put him on the longest contract in Scottish football, they demonstrated their confidence in him in the clearest manner.

Brian Hamilton

Born in Paisley, Brian won Scottish schools honours before joining St. Mirren from Pollok United BC. He was one of Alex Miller's starlets who won the Scottish Cup for the Paisley club, and had already convinced the Hibs' manager that he was well worth the £275,000 splashed out on him in the summer of 1989. A player of delicate touch, Brian took a little time to find his feet at Easter Road, but was a valuable member of the team, with further international recognition at under-21 level by the time his season ended abruptly with a broken leg at Ibrox.

Keith Houchen

Keith Houchen hails from Teesside, and played for Hartlepool, Orient, York City and Scunthorpe United before making the big time at Coventry; he won a Fourth Division medal with York, and scored with a spectacular header in Coventry's FA Cup win against Spurs. Passed the landmark of a century of league goals about five years ago. At six foot two, Keith is a threat to any defence in the air, but also shows an unusual amount of ball control on the ground for one so big. Hibs' top scorer in 1989-90, his first full season after signing for £300,000 from Coventry.

Gordon Hunter

Gordon Hunter joined Hibs from Musselburgh Windsor in 1983, and, a regular during the past five seasons, has matured into one of the most dependable defenders in the modern game. He quickly found international recognition at under-18 level, and more recently has given service to Andy Roxburgh's under-21 team. He is most frequently employed in the centre of defence, but has operated successfully at full-back too. Now 23 years of age.

Pat McGinlay

Signed from Blackpool in 1987 and now twenty-three years of age, Pat McGinlay is a real powerhouse in midfield, with the versatility which has seen him operate in central defence and as a striker too. His energy and ballwinning ability make him a suitable partner for the subtler skills of players like Brian Hamilton and Billy Findlay.

Mark McGraw

Hibs had to compete with Liverpool and Manchester United to sign Mark McGraw, and pay £175,000 for a youngster who had played just a handful of games for Morton in the First Division, but of whom great things are hoped. Mark's father Allan was an Easter Road favourite in the sixties, and Mark's manager at Greenock. Alex Miller was impressed by the teenager's touch and technique, although he is understandably short in experience - a position which was not helped when damaged ligaments ended his season prematurely!

Tommy McIntyre

Born in Lanarkshire in 1962, Tommy signed for Aberdeen from Fir Park BC in 1981, and was one of Alex Miller's first buys for Hibs - on Hogmanay 1986 - along with Graeme Mitchell and Dougie Bell. Holds a European Supercup medal gained while at Pittodrie. Equally at home in central defence or fullback, Tommy has an uncanny resemblance to erstwhile Easter Road favourite John Baxter.

Willie Miller

Twenty-year-old Willie Miller stepped into the Hibs' team at Parkhead in February 1990 with the assurance of a veteran, and has been a regular since. Signed from Edina Hibs in 1985, Willie is regarded by many as being the best prospect in his position since John Brownlie - Hibs obviously think so, and Willie is accordingly signed on a long-term contract.

Callum Milne

Born in Edinburgh in 1965, Callum joined Hibs from Salvesens BC and made his debut in 1984-85. A confident young fullback with a lot of skill on the ball, Callum played in about half the games in 1988-89, before injury curtailed his appearances last season. At five foot eight, Callum is not the biggest defender in the business, but compensates with tenacity and speed.

Graeme Mitchell

Graeme Mitchell was one of manager Miller's first signings for Hibs, on the last day of 1986 from Hamilton Accies, where he was captain, and where he won a First Division medal. A Glaswegian, Graeme is a strong unflappable player in central defence or sweeper, and has the pace and strength to play in midfield when occasion demands, notably in two outstanding performances against Videoton.

Neil Orr

Neil Orr was Hibs' first signing following David Duff's takeover, and made a scoring debut against Queen of the South in August 1987. Born in Airdrie, he made his debut for Morton in 1975-76, and won a number of under-21 caps before joining West Ham United in 1981. Hibs paid the Hammers £100,000 to bring him north. Equally at home in central defence, or midfield, where he has been seen most often in Hibs' colours.

Chris Reid

Another product of Hutchison Vale, Chris Reid came to Hibs as a sixteen-year-old in 1988 and last term signed a long-term contract, clear evidence of his manager's faith in him. This was more than justified last year when he deputised for Andy Goram in a couple of Premier League games, and again in the BP youth cup final against Dundee United. Has already a number of schoolboy and youth caps, and seems destined for a fine career.

Alan Sneddon

Now the longest-serving player at Easter Road with around 300 league appearances, Alan has given outstanding service to the club since Bertie Auld signed him from Celtic nearly ten years ago. He joined Celtic from Larkhall Thistle, won under-21 honours, and cup and league badges while at Parkhead, and a First Division medal in his first season here. He is nowadays seen more on the left than the right, and found time to contribute four goals last term.

Joe Tortolano

Joe Tortolano is a native of Stirling, but was signed from West Bromwich Albion where he had been an apprentice; Joe is a natural left winger, with plenty of pace, and one of the best crossers of a ball in the Premier League. More recently, he has been operating as an overlapping left back, and to such effect that he has won two under-21 caps in that role. Has been with Hibs since 1985.

Michael Weir

Pint-size Micky Weir joined Hibs from Portobello Thistle in 1982, and has always been a favourite with the Easter Road fans, with his infectious style of play and willingness to take on opponents. He joined Luton Town in 1987, but after just four months in England returned to the only club he has ever supported. Was prevented from gaining under-21 honours by illness and injury, but now fit again and approaching his best form.

Paul Wright

It was third time lucky for Hibs when they signed Paul Wright from QPR in March 1990 - but third time unlucky for the player when Hearts' Neil Berry ended his season in his third appearance for Hibs. Born in East Kilbride in 1967 and an under-21 cap with Aberdeen before going to London in 1989, Paul is expected to contribute goals and excitement to Hibs' attack this season, and manager Miller reckons him well worth the £300,000 he cost the club.

Gareth Evans

Despite his name, Gareth is English, having been born in Coventry in 1967. He joined the Highfield Road club as an apprentice, then after a handful of first team appearances, was transferred to Rotherham in 1986. He had scored thirteen goals in 63 league games when Hibs signed him in early 1988. Gareth's pace and enthusiasm, and a debut goal against Dundee, made him a valuable member of Alex Miller's pool, although it seems likely that his future will be closer to his roots.

Paul Kane

Paul was born in Edinburgh in 1965 from Salvesens BC, and is one of a clutch of Hibs' players whose fathers also wore the club's colours. Now Hibs' second most senior professional, Paul has given splendid service in defence, midfield and attack, and is the only current Hibs' man to have notched over thirty goals for the club. Paul made his debut at Tannadice in 1983-84 and has well over 200 league appearances to his credit.

Murdo MacLeod

Born in Glasgow in September 1958, Murdo signed for Dumbarton in 1974 from Glasgow Amateurs, and from there he moved to Celtic in 1978–79. At Parkhead, although playing midfield and defence, he contributed over fifty goals and won his first caps for Scotland. In 1987 he left for Borussia Dortmund; most commentators thought his career was now on a downslope, but MacLeod obtained the majority of his caps in Germany, and was nicknamed 'King of Dortmund'. Murdo has joined Hibs as a player and also assistant to Alex Miller.

HIBERNIAN DIRECTORS

FOOTBALL CLUB
JAMES C. GRAY (MANAGING)
RAYMOND M. SPARKES
JEREMY JAMES
CHARLES McCOLE
DOUGLAS W.M. CROMB
JOHN MULVEY
SHEILA ROWLAND
JAMES KERR (HONORARY)

PLC
ALISTER DOW (CHAIRMAN)
JEREMY JAMES
J.C. GRAY
TOM FARMER
TOM HARRISON
DEREK MORAN
ALLAN MUNRO
D.F. DUFF

MANAGERIAL STAFF

Alex Miller Manager

Andy Watson Coach
Stuart Collie Physiotherapist

HIBERNIAN YOUNGSTERS 1990-91

Lee Bailey	Edina Hibs	1989	Forward
Kenny Balmain	Eastercraigs	1990	Central defender
Paul Currie	Musselburgh Wr	1990	Defender
David Farrell	Oxford Utd	1988	Midfield/defence
Jason Gardner	Salvesens BC	1990	Goalkeeper
Nicky Ingram	Salvesens BC	1989	Forward
Chris Jackson	Salvesens BC	1990	Midfield
Danny Lennon	Hutchison Vale	1985	Midfield
Graeme Love	Salvesens BC	1989	Midfield
Colin McDonald	Musselburgh Wr	1990	Forward
Adrian Mckenna	Campsie BW	1989	Midfield
Graham Miller	Tynecastle BC	1990	Midfield
David Nicholls	Ferguslie Utd	1988	Defender
Stephen Raynes	Salvesens BC	1987	Midfield
Graeme Soutar	Salvesens BC	1990	Forward
Steven Tweed	Hutchison Vale	1989	Defender
Stephen Woods	Kilpatrick Juv	1989	Goalkeeper

Scottish Cup Record

1875–76	Hibs did not take part.			
1876–77	Hibs did not take part.			
1877–78	Rd. 1	v.	Hearts	0-0, 2-1
	2	v.	Hanover	1-1, 3-0
	3	v.	Swifts	2-0
	4	v.	Thornliebank (a)	*1-1, 2-2

* This is the score given in the Glasgow Daily News and is presumably that on which a replay was ordered.

	5	v.	South Western (a)	1-3
1878–79	Rd. 1	v.	Dunfermline (h)	5-2
	2	v.	3rd ERV (a)	3-0

abandoned because 3rd ERV were unable to continue

	3	v.	Edinburgh Univ. (a)	5-2
	4	v.	Rob Roy (h)	9-0
	5	v.	Helensburgh (h)	1-2
1879–80	Rd. 1	v.	Hanover (a)	5-1
	2	v.	Dunfermline (a)	4-0
	3	v.	Hearts (h)	2-1
	4	v.	Park Grove (h)	2-2, 2-2
	5	v.	Mauchline (a)	2-0
	6	v.	Dumbarton (a)	2-6
1880–81	Rd. 1	v.	bye	
	2	v.	Dunfermline (h)	3-1
	3	v.	Hearts (a)	3-5
1881–82	Rd. 1	v.	Addiewell (a)	7-0
	2	v.	St. Bernards (h)	2-1
	3	v.	bye	
	4	v.	West Benhar (a)	4-4, 8-0
	5	v.	Dumbarton (h)	*2-6, 2-6

* result protested.

1882-83	Rd. 1	v.	Brunswick (h)	8-0
	2	v.	West Calder (a)	3-2
	3	v.	bye	
	4	v.	Partick Thistle (h)	2-2, 4-1
	5	v.	Arthurlie (a)	*3-4, 0-6

* result protested

1883-84	Rd. 1	v.	West Calder (h)	5-0
	2	v.	Edina (h)	10-1
	3	v.	Hearts (a)	4-1
	4	v.	5th Kirkcudbright RV (a)	8-1
	5	v.	bye	

	6	v.	Battlefield (h)	6-1
	S	v.	Queens Park (h)	1-5
1884–85	Rd. 1	v.	Bo'ness	2-0
	2	v.	Vale of Teith (h)	5-1
	3	v	Glengowan (h)	5-1
	4	v.	Ayr (h)	4-1
	5	v.	Morton (h)	4-0
	6	v.	Annbank (h)	5-0
	S	v.	Renton (h)	2-3
1885–86	Rd. 1	v.	bye	
	2	v.	Hearts (h)	2-1
	3	v.	Bo'ness (h)	6-0
	4	v.	Arbroath (h)	5-3
	5	v.	Dumbarton (a)	2-2, 4-3
	6	v.	Cambuslang (h)	3-2
	S	v.	Renton (h)	0-2
1886–87	Rd. 1	v.	Durhamtown Rangers (h)	5-1
	2	v.	Mossend Swifts (a)	1-1, 3-0
	3	v.	Hearts (h)	5-1
	4	v.	bye	
	5	v.	Queen of the S. Wand. (h)	7-3
	6	v.	Third Lanark (a)	2-1
	S	v.	Vale of Leven (h)	3-1
	F	v.	Dumbarton (n)	2-1
1887–88	Rd. 1	v.	Broxburn Thistle (h)	5-0
	2	v.	Erin Rovers (a)	6-0
	3	v.	Hearts (a)	1-1, 1-3
1888–89	Rd. 1	v.	Mossend Swifts (a)	1-2
1889–90	Rd. 1	v.	Armadale (a)	3-2
	2	v.	Mossend Swifts (h)	4-3
	3	v.	Dunfermline Ath (a)	4-4, 11-1
	4	v.	Queen of the S. Wand. (a)	7-3
	5	v.	bye	
	6	v.	Abercorn (a)	2-6
1890–91	Rd. 1	v.	Kirkcaldy Wand. (a)	4-3
	2	v.	Dumbarton (h)	1-9
1891–92	Hibs did not take part.			
1892–93	Hibs did not take part.			
1893–94	(Qualfying Cup)			
	Rd. 1	v.	Cowdenbeath (a)	2-1
	2	v.	Broxburn (h)	5-0
	3	v.	Vale of Leven (a)	0-1

1894–95	Rd. 1	v.	Forfar Athletic (a)	6-1
	2	v.	Celtic (h)	*2-0, 0-2
	* result protested			
1895–96	Rd. 1	v.	E. Stirlingshire (a)	3-2
	2	v.	Raith Rovers (h)	6-1
	3	v.	Rangers (a)	3-2
	S	v.	Renton (h)	2-1
	F	v.	Hearts (n)	1-3
1896–97	Rd. 1	v.	Duncrub Park (a)	10-1
	2	v.	Rangers (a)	0-3
1897–98	Rd. 1	v.	Abercorn (a)	1-1, 7-1
	2	v.	E. Stirlingshire (h)	3-1
	3	v.	Third lanark (a)	0-2
1898–99	Rd. 1	v.	Royal Albert (h)	2-1
	2	v.	Queens Park (a)	1-5
1899–1900	Rd. 1	v.	Hamilton Acads. (a)	3-2
	2	v.	Hearts (a)	1-1, 1-2
1900–01	Rd. 1	v.	Dumbarton (h)	7-0
	2	v.	Royal Albert (a)	1-1, 1-0
	3	v.	Morton (h)	2-0
	S	v.	Hearts (a)	1-1, 1-2
1901–02	Rd. 1	v.	Clyde (h)	2-0
	2	v.	Port Glasgow Ath. (a)	5-1
	3	v.	Queens Park (a)	7-1
	S	v.	Rangers (a)	2-0
	F	v.	Celtic (a)	1-0
1902–03	Rd. 1	v.	Morton (h)	7-0
	2	v.	Leith Athletic (h)	4-1
	3	v.	Dundee (h)	0-0, 0-0, 0-1
1903–04	Rd. 1	v.	Airdrie (h)	2-1
	2	v.	Rangers (h)	1-2
1904–05	Rd. 1	v.	Partick Thistle (h)	1-1, 2-4
1905–06	Rd. 1	v.	Falkirk (a)	2-1
	2	v.	Partick Th (h)	1-1, 1-1, 2-1
	3	v.	Third Lanark (h)	2-3
1906–07	Rd. 1	v.	Forfat Ath (h)	5-0
	2	v.	Johnstone (h)	1-1, 5-0
	3	v.	St. Mirren (h)	1-1, 1-1, 2-0
	S	v.	Celtic (a)	0-0, 0-0, 0-3
1907–08	Rd. 1	v.	Abercorn (h)	5-0
	2	v.	Morton (h)	3-0
	3	v.	Kilmarnock (h)	0-1

1808–09	Rd. 1	v.	Ayr (h)	2-1
	2	v.	Clyde (a)	0-1
1909–10	Rd. 1	v.	Hamilton Acads. (a)	0-0, 2-0
	2	v.	Ayr (a)	1-0
	3	v.	Hearts (h)	*0-1, 1-0

* taken as a draw after abandonment following break-in.

	S	v.	Dundee (h)	0-0, 0-0, 0-1
1910–11	Rd. 1	v.	Dundee (a)	1-2
1911–12	Rd. 1	v.	Hearts (a)	0-0, 1-1, 1-3
1912–13	Rd. 1	v.	bye	
	2	v.	Motherwell (a)	1-1, 0-0, 2-1
	3	v.	Raith Rovers (a)	2-2, 0-1
1913–14	Rd. 1	v.	bye	
	2	v.	Morton (a)	1-1, 2-1
	3	v.	Rangers (h)	2-1
	4	v.	Queens Park (a)	3-1
	S	v.	St. Mirren (n)	3-1
	F	v.	Celtic (n)	0-0, 1-4
1914–19	No competition			
1919–20	Rd. 1	v.	Calston (a)	0-0, 2-1
	2	v.	Armadale (a)	0-1
1920–21	Rd. 1	v.	Th. Lanark (a)	1-1, 1-1, 1-0
	2	v.	Partick Th. (a)	0-0, 0-0, 0-1
1921–22	Rd. 1	v.	Armadale (h)	3-0
	2	v.	Motherwell (a)	2-3
1922–23	Rd. 1	v.	Clackmannan (h)	4-0
	2	v.	Peebles Rovers (h)	0-0, 3-0
	3	v.	Queens Park (h)	2-0
	4	v.	Aberdeen (h)	2-0
	S	v.	Third Lanark (n)	0-1
	F	v.	Celtic (n)	0-1
1923–24	Rd. 1	v.	Dundee United (h)	1-0
	2	v.	Alloa Ath. (h)	1-1, 5-0
	3	v.	Rangers (a)	2-1
	4	v.	Partick Th. (h)	2-2, 1-1, 2-1
	S	v.	Aberdeen (n)	0-0, 0-0, 1-0
	F	v.	Airdrie (n)	0-2
1924–25	Rd. 1	v.	Aberdeen (h)	0-2
1925–26	Rd. 1	v.	Broxburn Utd. (h)	1-1, 1-0
	2	v.	Airdrie (h)	2-3
1926–27	Rd. 1	v.	Dykehead	w.c.

	2	v.	Third Lanark (a)	2-0
	3	v.	Falkirk (h)	0-0, 1-0
	4	v.	Dunfermline Ath (a)	4-0
	S	v.	Rangers (n)	0-3
1928–29	Rd. 1	v.	St. Johnstone (h)	1-2
1929–30	Rd. 1	v.	Leith Amateurs (h)	2-0
	2	v.	Ayr United (a)	3-1
	3	v.	Hearts (h)	1-3
1930–31	Rd. 1	v.	St. Cuthbert Wand (h)	3-1
	2	v.	Hamilton Acads. (a)	2-2, 5-2
	3	v.	Motherwell (h)	0-3
1931–32	Rd. 1	v.	Dundee United (h)	2-3
1932–33	Rd. 1	v.	Forfar Athletic (h)	2-2, 7-3
	2	v.	Aberdeen (a)	1-1. 1-0
	3	v.	bye	
	4	v.	Hearts (h)	0-0, 0-2
1933–34	Rd. 1	v.	Clyde (h)	5-4
	2	v.	Alloa Athletic (h)	6-0
	3	v.	Aberdeen (h)	0-1
1934–35	Rd. 1	v.	Vale of Atholl (h)	5-0
	2	v.	Clachnacuddin (h)	7-1
	3	v.	Aberdeen (a)	0-0, 1-1, 2-3
1935–36	Rd. 1	v.	Vale Acoba (a)	3-1
	2	v.	Clyde (a)	1-4
1936–37	Rd. 1	v.	Alloa Athletic (a)	5-2
	2	v.	Hamilton Acads. (a)	1-2
1937–38	Rd. 1	v.	Edinburgh City (a)	2-3
1938–39	Rd. 1	v.	Forfar Athletic (a)	3-0
	2	v.	Kilmarnock (h)	3-1
	3	v.	bye	
	4	v.	Alloa Athletic (h)	3-1
	S	v.	Clyde (n)	0-1
1939–46	No competition.			
1946–47	Rd. 1	v.	Alloa Athletic (a)	8-0
	2	v.	bye	
	3	v.	Rangers (a)	0-0, 2-0
	4	v.	Dumbarton (h)	2-0
	S	v.	Motherwell (n)	2-1
	F	v.	Aberdeen (n)	1-2
1947–48	Rd. 1	v.	Albion Rovers (a)	2-0
	2	v.	Arbroath (h)	4-0

	3	v.	Aberdeen (h)	4-2
	4	v.	St. Mirren (h)	3-1
	S	v.	Rangers (n)	0-1
1948–49	Rd. 1	v.	Forfar Athletic (a)	4-0
	2	v.	Raith Rovers (h)	1-1, 4-3
	3	v.	bye	
	4	v.	East Fife (h)	0-2
1949–50	Rd. 1	v.	Partick Thistle (h)	0-1
1950–51	Rd. 1	v.	St. Mirren (a)	1-1, 5-0
	2	v.	Rangers (a)	3-2
	3	v.	bye	
	4	v.	Airdrie (a)	3-0
	S	v.	Motherwell (n)	2-3
1951–52	Rd. 1	v.	Raith Rovers (a)	0-0, 0-0, 1-4
1952–53	Rd. 1	v.	Stenhousemuir (h)	8-1
	2	v.	Queens Park (h)	4-2
	3	v.	Aberdeen (h)	1-1, 0-2
1953–54	Rd. 1	v.	St. Johnstone (a)	2-1
	2	v.	Clyde (h)	7-0
	3	v.	Aberdeen (h)	1-3
1954–55	Rd. 5	v.	Hearts (a)	0-5
1955–56	Rd. 5	v.	Raith Rovers (h)	1-1, 1-3
1956–57	Rd. 5	v.	Aberdeen (h)	3-4
1957–58	Rd. 1	v.	Dundee United (a)	0-0, 2-0
	2	v.	Hearts (a)	4-3
	3	v.	Third Lanark (h)	3-2
	S	v.	Rangers (n)	2-2, 2-1
	F	v.	Clyde (n)	0-1
1958–59	Rd. 1	v.	Raith Rovers (a)	1-1, 2-1
	2	v.	Falkirk (h)	3-1
	3	v.	Partick Thistle (h)	3-1
	4	v.	Third Lanark (a)	1-2
1959–60	Rd. 1	v.	bye	
	2	v.	Dundee (h)	3-0
	3	v.	East Stirling (a)	3-0
	4	v.	Rangers (a)	2-3
1960–61	Rd. 1	v.	Clyde (a)	2-0
	2	v.	Peebles Rovers (h)	15-1
	3	v.	Hamilton Acads. (a)	4-0
	4	v.	Celtic (a)	1-1, 0-1
1961–62	Rd. 1	v.	Partick This. (a)	2-2, 2-3

1962–63	Rd.1	v.	bye	
	2	v.	Brechin City (a)	2-0
	3	v.	Dundee (a)	0-1
1963–64	Rd.1	v.	Aberdeen (a)	2-5
1964–65	Rd.1	v.	E.S. Clydebank (h)	1-1, 2-0
	2	v.	Partick Thistle (h)	5-1
	3	v.	Rangers (h)	2-1
	S	v.	Dunfermline Ath. (n)	0-2
1965–66	Rd.1	v.	Third Lanark (h)	4-3
	2	v.	Hearts (a)	1-2
1966–67	Rd.1	v.	Brechin City (h)	2-0
	2	v.	Berwick Rangers (h)	1-0
	3	v.	Aberdeen (h)	1-1, 0-3
1967–68	Rd.1	v.	East Stirling (a)	5-3
	2	v.	Airdrie (a)	0-1
1968–69	Rd.1	v.	Rangers (a)	0-1
1969–70	Rd.1	v.	Rangers (a)	1-3
1970–71	Rd.3	v.	Forfar Athletic (h)	8-1
	4	v.	Hearts (a)	2-1
	5	v.	Dundee (h)	1-0
	S	v.	Rangers (n)	0-0, 1-2
1971–72	Rd.3	v.	Partick Thistle (a)	2-0
	4	v.	Airdrie (h)	2-0
	5	v.	Aberdeen (h)	2-0
	S	v.	Rangers (n)	1-1, 2-0
	F	v.	Celtic (n)	1-6
1972–73	Rd.3	v.	Morton (h)	2-0
	4	v.	Rangers (a)	1-1, 1-2
1973–74	Rd.3	v.	Kilmarnock (h)	5-2
	4	v.	Dundee (h)	3-3, 0-3
1974–75	Rd.3	v.	Celtic (h)	0-2
1975–76	Rd.3	v.	Dunfermline Ath. (h)	3-2
	4	v.	Dundee United (h)	1-1, 2-0
	5	v.	Motherwell (a)	2-2, 1-1, 1-2
1976–77	Rd.3	v.	Partick Thistle (h)	3-0
	4	v.	Arbroath (a)	1-1, 1-2
1977–78	Rd.3	v.	East Fife (h)	4-0
	4	v.	Partick Thistle (h)	0-0, 1-2
1978–79	Rd.3	v.	Dunfermline Ath (a)	1-1, 2-0
	4	v.	Meadowbank Thistle (a)	6-0
	5	v.	Hearts (h)	2-1

	S	v.	Aberdeen (n)	2-1
	F	v.	Rangers (n)	0-0, 0-0, 2-3
1979–80	Rd. 3	v.	Meadowbank Thistle (a)	1-0
	4	v.	Ayr United (h)	2-0
	5	v.	Berwick Rangers (a)	0-0, 1-0
	S	v.	Celtic (n)	0-5
1980–81	Rd. 3	v.	Dunfermline Ath (h)	1-1, 2-1
	4	v.	Falkirk (h)	1-0
	5	v.	Rangers (a)	1-3
1981–81	Rd. 3	v.	Falkirk (h)	2-0
	4	v.	Dundee Utd. (a)	1-1. 1-1. 0-3
1982–83	Rd. 3	v.	Aberdeen (h)	1-4
1983–84	Rd. 3	v.	East Fife (h)	0-0, 0-2
1984–85	Rd. 3	v.	Dundee United (a)	0-3
1985–86	Rd. 3	v.	Dunfermline Ath. (h)	2-0
	4	v.	Ayr United (h)	1-0
	5	v.	Celtic (h)	4-3
	S	v.	Aberdeen (n)	0-3
1986–87	Rd. 3	v.	Denfermline Ath. (h)	2-0
	4	v.	Clydebank (a)	0-1
1987–88	Rd. 3	v.	Dumbarton (a)	0-0, 3-0
	4	v.	Celtic (a)	0-0, 0-1
1988–89	Rd. 3	v.	Breching City (h)	1-0
	4	v.	Motherwell (h)	2-1
	5	v.	Alloa Athletic (h)	1-0
	S	v.	Celtic (n)	1-3
1989–90	Rd. 3	v.	Brechin City (a)	2-0
	4	v.	East Fife (h)	5-1
	5	v.	Dundee United (a)	0-1

League Record

	2nd Division		1st Division		
	1893-94	1894-95	1895-96	1896-97	1897-98
Abercorn	7-2, 3-3	4-2, 5-1		9-0, 2-2	
Airdrie		6-1, 4-2			
Celtic			4-2, 3-1	3-1, 1-1	1-2, 1-4
Clyde	4-3, 4-0		4-3, 3-0	5-1, 7-0	5-0, 4-2
Cowlairs	3-4, 3-2	8-2, 8-2			
Dumbarton			7-2, 3-1		
Dundee			3-1, 2-2	3-1, 0-3	2-0, 1-1
Dundee Wands.		8-2, 6-0			
Glasgow This.	4-0, 2-1				
Hearts			3-2, 3-4	2-0, 0-1	1-1, 2-3
Morton	9-2, 1-0	6-3, 7-1			
Motherwell	8-2, 1-2	5-0, 0-2			
Northern	6-0, 2-2				
Partick This.	6-1, 7-1	5-1, 4-0			4-2, 3-0
Pt. Glasgow Ath.	10-1, 3-3	3-3, 2-2			
Rangers			1-1, 0-4	4-3, 3-4	0-5, 0-1
Renton		9-1, 2-3			
St. Bernards			2-3, 5-2	2-0, 1-0	6-1, 2-3
St. Mirren			5-1, 3-1	3-0, 0-2	3-1, 3-2
Third Lanark			2-5, 7-2	2-0, 3-1	6-0, 3-1

First Division

	1889-99	1899-00	1900-01	1901-02	1902-03
Celtic	2-1, 2-1	1-1, 1-2	2-2, 1-3	1-2, 2-2	1-1, 4-0
Clyde	2-1, 2-2	5-0, 4-3			
Dundee	5-0, 4-2	3-3, 2-2	2-1, 3-1	5-0, 0-1	1-0, 3-0
Hearts	1-5, 0-4	1-0, 3-1	3-0, 0-0	1-2, 1-2	0-0, 1-1
Kilmarnock		3-1, 3-0	2-2, 2-2	5-0, 0-0	2-1, 4-1
Morton			1-1, 0-1	1-2, 2-0	3-1, 1-0
Partick This.	1-1, 4-1		2-0, 1-0		2-2, 2-0
Pt. Glasgow Ath.					5-1, 1-0
Queens Park			0-1, 1-1	8-1, 0-2	3-2, 3-1
Rangers	3-4, 0-10	0-2, 2-3	4-1, 0-6	2-3, 2-0	1-0, 5-2
St. Bernards	4-3, 3-1	1-1, 4-0			
St. Mirren	4-3, 0-2	5-1, 1-1	1-0, 2-0	1-2, 1-1	4-3, 1-1
Third Lanark	1-1, 4-1	3-2, 1-1	2-0, 0-0	2-2, 2-1	1-0, 0-1

First Division

	1903-04	1904-05	1905-06	1906-07	1907-08	1908-09
Aberdeen			1-0, 1-2	2-1, 1-1	1-0, 1-1	2-1, 0-4
Airdrie	4-0, 2-0	3-2, 1-1	0-4, 0-2	4-0, 2-3	4-0, 2-0	2-0, 1-2
Celtic	0-2, 0-1	2-2, 0-2	0-1, 0-1	0-1, 0-2	1-2, 0-4	1-0, 0-2
Clyde				2-0, 1-3	2-1, 1-1	1-1, 0-2
Dundee	0-1, 2-1	1-1, 1-4	2-1, 1-1	0-4, 0-0	0-1, 1-0	0-1, 0-3
Falkirk			4-1, 1-2	1-2, 1-2	0-4, 1-3	2-0, 0-0
Hamilton Acads.				4-2, 0-1	2-5, 1-1	2-0, 1-1
Hearts	2-4, 0-2	3-0, 0-1	0-3, 0-1	0-0, 1-4	2-3, 2-1	0-1, 1-1
Kilmarnock	2-2, 0-0	2-1, 1-2	2-1, 2-0	1-0, 3-1	3-1, 0-3	2-1, 1-0
Morton	2-0, 1-3	4-0, 2-2	1-2, 1-0	2-1, 1-2	3-0, 3-0	3-0, 0-3
Motherwell	2-1, 0-1	2-0, 2-1	2-3, 2-0	1-1, 0-0	1-1, 0-0	4-1, 0-1
Partick This.	2-2, 1-3	4-0, 1-0	1-1, 0-1	2-2, 0-3	6-0, 1-1	1-1, 5-1
Pt. Glasgow Ath.	4-1, 1-3	1-1, 1-1	3-1, 0-0	1-0, 2-1	2-1, 3-1	1-1, 2-1
Queens Park	1-3, 1-1	1-1, 2-4	4-0, 2-2	2-1, 0-0	4-1, 2-1	1-0, 1-0
Rangers	1-2, 1-1	1-2, 0-4	1-2, 1-1	1-3, 0-1	0-3, 1-1	1-0, 0-0
St. Mirren	2-1, 0-3	2-0, 0-2	0-1, 0-2	2-2, 1-1	2-1, 1-0	2-1, 0-1
Third Lanark	0-2, 0-2	1-1, 1-4	2-1, 1-3	1-1, 0-0	2-0, 0-0	3-0, 0-1

First Division

	1909-10	1910-11	1911-12	1912-13	1913-14
Aberdeen	1-2, 0-1	2-1, 1-1	1-1, 1-1	3-1, 3-1	1-0, 2-1
Airdrie	3-0, 2-0	2-0, 0-3	2-1, 0-1	2-2, 0-1	1-4, 3-4
Ayr United					0-5, 2-1
Celtic	1-0, 0-0	0-4, 0-2	1-1, 1-3	1-0, 1-1	1-2, 0-3
Clyde	0-1, 1-2	1-1, 0-2	1-2, 0-1	3-1, 0-2	1-1, 0-4
Dumbarton					1-1, 3-0
Dundee	0-0, 2-4	4-1, 1-1	2-1, 2-3	4-0, 2-2	4-1, 2-2
Falkirk	1-1, 0-2	1-2, 1-2	5-0, 0-1	3-3, 2-0	0-3, 2-3
Hamilton Acads.	1-0, 1-1	2-1, 1-1	1-0, 0-3	3-1, 1-3	6-0, 1-0
Hearts	1-4, 0-1	1-0, 0-2	0-4, 0-3	0-3, 0-1	1-2, 1-3
Kilmarnock	2-1, 0-4	0-1, 1-3	0-1, 2-1	4-0, 1-0	0-1, 3-0
Morton	2-1, 0-2	3-3, 2-2	1-2, 1-2	3-1, 3-0	1-2, 1-2
Motherwell	1-0, 1-3	2-1, 2-1	1-0, 2-0	1-2, 1-5	2-0, 3-2
Partick This.	3-1, 1-3	1-0, 1-2	4-0, 0-3	1-0, 2-1	0-2, 0-3
Pt. Glasgow Ath.	2-1, 2-0				
Queens Park	1-0, 2-1	1-0, 1-0	2-0, 0-2	3-0, 5-3	2-3, 2-4
Raith Rovers		2-0, 3-1	3-0, 2-2	1-2, 2-4	0-3, 1-1
Rangers	1-0, 0-1	1-3, 0-4	5-0, 0-2	0-1, 3-5	0-3, 1-1
St. Mirren	0-0, 0-3	2-0, 0-2	0-0, 1-2	1-1, 3-0	5-3, 3-3
Third Lanark	0-0, 1-0	2-1, 3-0	3-2, 0-2	1-4, 0-3	1-0, 1-2

First Division

	1914-15	1915-16	1916-17	1917-18	1918-19
Aberdeen	1-2, 0-0	0-0, 1-1	3-3, 1-2		
Ardrie	1-0, 3-1	3-0, 0-1	1-1, 1-3	2-1. 0-3	2-1, 3-3
Ayr United	0-4, 1-2	3-1, 3-2	1-4, 1-2	1-1, 2-2	0-1, 0-5
Celtic	1-1, 1-5	0-4, 1-3	0-1, 1-3	0-2, 0-2	0-3, 0-2
Clyde	3-1, 0-1	0-1, 1-2	1-1, 2-1	2-0, 5-2	3-1, 1-2
Clydebank				0-1, 0-2	1-2, 1-2
Dumbarton	2-2, 0-1	1-1, 1-2	3-1, 1-2	0-3, 0-1	1-0, 0-4
Dundee	2-0, 4-2	0-2, 1-2	1-2, 1-3		
Falkirk	1-1, 0-0	2-1, 1-1	1-2, 1-0	2-1, 2-2	2-1, 1-1
Hamilton Acads.	0-2, 2-2	1-3, 2-3	4-3, 1-4	1-1, 0-1	1-2, 0-1
Hearts	2-2, 1-3	3-1, 1-2	0-2, 1-2	1-3, 0-1	1-3, 1-3
Kilmarnock	3-1, 1-5	1-0. 0-0	2-1, 3-1	0-3, 1-3	1-4, 1-7
Morton	1-1, 0-0	0-2, 1-5	2-4, 1-1	2-2, 1-1	0-3, 2-9
Motherwell	1-2, 0-3	1-2, 1-1	2-3, 1-1	2-2, 1-2	0-3, 0-0
Partick This.	4-1, 1-3	0-4, 1-4	1-0, 3-0	2-1, 2-2	0-2, 0-2
Queens Park	4-0, 2-0	3-0, 2-4	5-1, 1-4	4-2, 0-2	1-0, 0-3
Raith Rovers	2-1, 1-1	1-0, 1-1	3-3, 1-2		
Rangers	1-2, 2-4	2-3, 2-4	0-0. 1-5	0-1, 0-3	1-2, 1-5
St. Mirren	3-2, 2-4	2-1, 1-3	2-1, 1-1	3-1, 1-1	1-2, 1-3
Third Lanark	4-2, 2-2	0-1, 0-3	1-1, 1-1	4-1, 0-1	1-5, 2-4

First Division

	1919-20	1920-21	1921-22	1922-23	1923 -24	1924 -25
Aberdeen	2-1, 1-1	2-3, 1-0	0-1, 2-1	2-0, 0-2	0-1, 1-1	4-1, 1-0
Airdrie	1-4, 0-2	0-2, 1-5	0-0, 1-2	1-0, 1-2	2-0, 1-1	1-1, 0-2
Albion Rovers	0-1, 2-1	5-2, 2-0	0-0, 1-2	3-0, 2-1		
Alloa				2-1, 1-2		
Ayr United	1-2, 0-1	3-2, 1-2	1-1, 2-2	3-0, 1-1	3-0, 2-2	7-0, 2-2
Celtic	1-2, 3-7	0-3, 0-3	2-1, 1-3	1-0, 0-0	0-0, 1-1	2-3, 1-1
Clyde	1-0, 0-2	0-1, 0-2	2-1, 0-2	1-2, 0-0	3-1, 0-2	
Clydebank	2-0, 3-3	1-1, 2-2	6-0, 2-0		3-2, 4-2	
Cowdenbeath						4-1, 1-1
Dumbarton	3-3, 0-2	2-0, 0-1	0-0, 1-1			
Dundee	0-0, 1-3	2-0, 1-1	1-1, 0-0	3-3, 0-1	2-0, 2-7	4-2, 0-3
Falkirk	2-0, 0-3	0-0, 0-3	1-1, 1-3	1-0, 0-5	1-0, 1-1	1-2, 0-0
Hamilton Acads.	3-0, 2-3	0-1, 1-1	1-0, 2-1	2-0, 1-2	1-3, 1-2	2-1, 2-0
Hearts	2-4, 3-1	3-0, 1-5	2-1, 2-0	2-1, 2-2	1-1, 1-1	2-1, 0-2
Kilmarnock	4-1, 1-4	0-0, 3-1	3-0, 1-1	1-1, 0-1	3-1, 1-2	2-0, 1-0
Morton	1-0, 1-1	4-0, 1-1	2-1, 2-2	0-1, 0-1	2-1, 0-1	2-0, 2-2
Motherwell	0-1, 2-3	2-3, 2-4	2-0, 1-4	2-1, 2-0	2-4, 1-2	1-0, 1-1
Partick This	6-2, 0-1	2-0, 2-3	2-0, 0-2	1-0, 0-1	3-1, 0-1	3-2, 1-3
Queens Park	3-2, 2-2	0-2, 2-0	3-0, 3-1		4-0, 1-1	2-0, 0-1
Raith Rovers	2-0. 0-1	1-1, 0-2	2-1, 0-0	2-0, 2-2	4-0, 2-0	3-0, 3-1
Rangers	1-1, 0-7	1-1, 0-1	0-0, 0-2	2-0, 0-2	1-3, 1-2	4-1, 0-3
St. Johnstone						5-0, 3-2
St. Mirren	2-1, 1-2	1-0, 2-0	1-1, 1-1	0-3, 1-2	1-1, 1-1	2-0, 2-2
Third Lanark	1-2, 0-2	2-1, 2-0	0-1, 1-2	2-0, 1-0	5-2, 4-1	5-1, 2-1

First Division

	1925-26	1926-27	1927-28	1928-29	1929-30	1930-31
Aberdeen	0-0, 0-5	2-3, 5-2	0-0, 2-4	4-1, 1-0	0-1, 0-2	1-2, 0-7
Airdrie	1-4, 1-5	2-1. 0-3	2-3, 2-2	1-1, 2-0	3-1, 0-3	2-0, 1-4
Ayr United				2-2, 1-4	1-0, 2-3	2-0, 3-1
Bo'ness			3-0, 1-2			
Celtic	4-4, 0-5	3-2, 3-2	2-2, 0-3	2-1, 4-1	0-2, 0-4	0-0, 0-6
Clyde		3-0, 0-2	0-1, 2-0	3-0, 1-0	1-1, 2-0	1-2, 2-3
Clydebank	5-1, 1-0					
Cowdenbeath	1-2, 1-3	2-0, 0-2	3-0, 1-3	1-2, 0-2	1-1, 0-0	1-0, 1-2
Dundee	2-1, 4-1	0-1, 0-3	4-0, 1-4	2-0, 0-1	0-1, 0-4	2-3, 0-1
Dundee United	3-5, 2-2	3-2, 2-0			3-0, 2-2	
Dunfermline Ath.		2-2, 2-4	3-3, 2-0			
East Fife						2-1, 0-1
Falkirk	3-1, 1-1	1-0, 0-2	3-1, 2-2	3-2, 1-2	1-0, 1-1	5-2, 2-2
Hamilton Acads.	8-4, 0-1	3-1, 1-0	5-1, 1-4	0-1, 1-2	1-2, 2-3	1-0. 0-1
Hearts	0-0, 4-1	2-2, 2-2	2-1, 2-2	1-0, 1-1	1-1, 1-1	2-2, 1-4
Kilmarnock	8-0, 1-2	5-1, 0-4	3-1, 1-2	1-1, 0-1	0-0, 1-3	3-2, 0-4
Leith Athletic						0-1, 1-1
Morton	4-1, 5-2	1-1, 0-3			0-1, 2-3	1-1, 4-5
Motherwell	3-1, 1-2	1-1, 1-2	2-2, 1-2	1-1, 1-3	1-1, 0-3	2-2, 0-6
Partick This.	3-4, 1-2	3-2, 1-5	4-1, 0-3	3-1, 0-3	3-0, 0-0	0-3, 0-1
Queens Park	1-2, 0-2	2-0, 4-3	6-2, 2-6	1-2, 1-6	6-3, 0-2	4-2, 2-2
Raith Rovers	2-0, 0-1		3-2, 0-3	2-0, 0-1		
Rangers	0-2, 1-3	2-2, 0-2	2-1, 1-4	1-2, 0-3	0-2, 0-3	1-2, 0-1
St. Johnstone	0-3, 0-0	1-5, 0-0	2-2, 0-2	2-2, 0-4	3-1, 3-4	
St. Mirren	0-2, 1-2	2-1, 1-3	1-1, 2-3	3-5, 0-1	2-2, 2-1	2-3, 0-1
Third Lanark				6-1, 1-2		

Second Division

	1931-32	1932-33
Albion Rovers	4-1, 0-1	2-1, 0-2
Alloa Athletic	1-0, 2-1	1-0, 3-0
Arbroath	3-1, 3-3	2-0, 3-0
Armadale	1-0, 1-1	8-2, 4-2 *
Bo'ness	2-1, 2-2	7-0, *
Brechin City	4-0, 3-3	3-1, 4-2
Dumbarton	0-1, 2-0	1-0, 2-3
Dunfermline Ath.	6-2, 1-1	3-1, 4-2
Dundee United		2-0, 2-0
East Fife	3-2, 1-1	2-1, 5-0
East Stirling	1-1, 1-4	
Edinburgh City	3-1, 1-2	7-1, 4-0
Forfar Athletic	5-1, 0-1	2-0, 3-3
Kings Park	2-1, 4-1	0-1, 0-0
Leith Athletic		3-0, 1-0
Montrose	0-0, 1-0	4-1, 3-1
Queen of the South	1-4, 3-2	1-2, 0-0
Raith Rovers	0-1, 2-1	2-1, 2-1
St. Bernards	2-4, 0-1	4-1, 1-0
St. Johnstone	6-0, 1-2	
Stenhousemuir	0-2, 1-2	4-1, 2-3

* These games were not included in the official table following the expulsion of Armadale and Bo'ness during the season.

First Division

	1933-34	1934-35	1935-36	1936-37	1937-38	1938-39
Aberdeen	3-2, 1-2	2-3, 0-2	1-4, 1-3	1-3, 1-1	1-1, 0-5	5-0, 1-6
Airdrie	0-2, 3-0	2-2, 0-7	2-3, 2-3			
Albion Rovers		3-3, 0-2	3-0, 1-0	1-1, 0-4		1-2, 1-0
Arbroath			0-2, 2-3	4-1, 0-1	5-0, 3-3	1-1, 4-2
Ayr United	0-0, 1-4	1-1, 1-1	0-1, 0-3		3-0, 1-1	2-3, 1-3
Celtic	1-2, 1-2	3-2, 0-4	0-5, 1-4	2-2, 1-5	0-3, 0-3	1-0, 4-5
Clyde	3-0, 0-1	4-0, 2-3	1-1, 4-7	0-1, 3-1	6-3, 1-1	1-1, 0-3
Cowdenbeath	6-1, 4-2					
Dundee	2-1, 0-1	2-1, 2-0	2-1, 1-2	0-0, 1-3	2-1, 2-1	
Dunfermline Ath.		3-1, 1-2	2-3, 1-0	0-0, 3-2		
Falkirk	1-3, 1-3	2-0, 2-5		2-2, 1-4	2-4, 0-0	3-0, 1-1
Hamilton Acads.	1-2, 1-4	3-1, 1-2	3-2, 3-2	5-4, 1-4	1-1, 0-4	2-2, 1-4
Hearts	1-4, 0-0	1-0, 2-5	1-1, 3-8	3-3, 2-3	2-2, 2-3	4-0, 1-0
Kilmarnock	4-1, 0-2	1-0, 1-0	3-1, 1-0	0-0, 2-3	1-1, 3-0	0-1, 1-0
Morton					4-2, 4-2	
Motherwell	0-2, 1-2	1-1, 1-4	2-3, 1-1	1-2, 4-3	1-1, 0-1	2-1, 2-3
Partick This.	0-2, 2-3	2-0, 1-3	2-0, 1-2	2-2, 1-3	2-1, 0-4	1-2, 0-4
Queen of the South	0-2, 0-1	1-1, 2-0	3-0, 1-1	2-2, 0-1	2-0, 2-3	2-3, 1-2
Queens Park	2-1, 1-2	5-1, 1-3	0-1, 1-6	2-3, 0-2	0-2, 1-1	3-1, 2-3
Raith Rovers						2-1, 2-1
Rangers	0-0, 0-6	1-2, 2-4	1-1, 0-3	1-4, 0-4	0-0, 0-2	1-1, 2-5
St. Johnstone	2-6, 1-0	1-1, 0-2	0-2, 2-2	3-3, 1-3	2-2, 0-2	5-2, 1-2
St. Mirren	2-1, 3-0	0-0, 2-1		0-0, 3-1	2-1, 0-1	6-1, 0-0
Third Lanark	3-1, 0-1		3-0, 1-1	0-1, 1-1	2-2, 0-1	1-1, 0-2

First Division

	1946-47	1947-48	1948-49	1949-50	1950-51	1951-52
Aberdeen	1-1, 1-2	4-0, 2-0	4-1, 2-1	2-0, 3-0	6-2, 1-2	4-4, 2-1
Airdrie		7-1, 3-0			5-0, 1-2	4-0, 2-0
Albion Rovers			4-4, 3-0			
Celtic	2-0, 1-4	1-1, 4-2	1-2, 2-1	4-1, 2-2	3-1, 1-0	3-1, 1-1
Clyde	1-0, 2-2	2-1, 2-2	3-0, 5-3	6-3, 1-0	1-0, 4-0	
Dundee		2-1, 1-3	2-1, 3-4	4-2, 2-1	2-0, 2-2	3-1, 4-1
East Fife			5-2, 3-2	4-1, 1-1	2-0, 2-1	4-2, 1-3
Falkirk	2-2, 3-2	2-0, 1-3	2-0, 1-1	5-1, 2-1	6-0, 5-1	
Hamilton Acads.	3-2, 0-0					
Hearts	0-1, 3-2	3-1, 1-2	3-1, 2-3	1-2, 2-5	0-1, 1-2	2-3, 1-1
Kilmarnock	6-0, 5-3					
Morton	1-1, 2-0	1-1, 2-1	3-4, 2-3		2-0, 4-2	1-0, 1-2
Motherwell	1-2, 1-2	5-0, 2-0	5-1, 1-5	6-1, 3-1	3-1, 6-2	3-1, 1-3
Partick This.	5-1, 2-0	1-0, 1-1	2-1, 6-2	2-0, 2-2	1-1, 0-0	5-0, 2-1
Queen of the South	9-1, 3-1	6-0, 3-0	1-1, 1-1	2-0, 2-2		5-0, 2-5
Queens Park	3-1, 1-0	4-0, 3-2				
Raith Rovers				4-2, 6-0	3-0, 3-1	5-0, 2-0
Rangers	1-1, 2-1	1-0, 1-2	0-1, 4-2	0-1, 0-0	4-1, 1-1	1-1, 2-2
St. Mirren	1-0, 1-0	5-0, 4-2	1-1, 0-2	5-0, 3-1	3-1, 1-0	5-0, 4-0
Stirling Albion				4-1, 5-3		8-0, 4-1
Third Lanark	4-1, 2-0	8-0, 4-1	1-0, 2-3	0-1, 2-0	3-1, 2-1	5-2, 5-0

First Division

	1952-53	1953-54	1954-55	1955-56	1956-57	1957-58
Aberdeen	3-0, 1-1	3-0, 3-1	0-1, 1-3	1-3, 2-6	4-1, 1-3	0-1, 1-0
Airdrie	3-1, 7-3	8-1, 2-2		3-3, 1-3	6-0, 3-5	4-0, 4-1
Ayr United					3-0, 3-2	
Celtic	1-1, 3-1	0-3, 2-2	0-5, 2-1	2-3, 3-0	3-3, 1-2	0-1, 0-4
Clyde	5-1, 3-2	4-0, 6-3	2-3, 3-6	1-0, 2-2		1-3, 1-2
Dundee	3-0, 0-2	2-0, 0-1	3-1, 2-2	6-3, 2-3	1-1, 3-0	1-1, 0-3
Dunfermline Ath.				7-1, 1-2	0-0, 3-1	
East Fife	2-1, 5-3	2-1, 3-1	0-0, 5-1	5-1, 2-1	4-0, 6-1	0-1, 3-2
Falkirk	4-2, 3-1	2-3, 4-2	0-1, 1-3	2-0, 0-2	6-1, 1-0	3-3, 3-1
Hamilton Acads.		4-1, 6-2				
Hearts	3-1, 2-1	1-2, 0-4	2-3, 1-5	2-2, 1-0	2-3, 2-0	0-2, 1-3
Kilmarnock			3-2, 3-0	2-1, 1-0	0-0, 1-2	1-2, 4-1
Motherwell	7-2, 7-3		4-1, 5-1	7-0, 1-1	1-1, 0-3	2-1, 1-3
Partick This.	1-1, 4-5	1-2, 2-0	3-1, 3-0	5-1, 1-1	2-0, 0-3	5-1, 0-2
Queen of the South	1-3, 7-2	1-0, 2-3	1-1, 2-0	4-1, 3-1	1-1, 0-2	1-2, 0-3
Queens Park					1-1, 1-2	2-0, 2-1
Raith Rovers	4-1, 2-4	5-0, 0-4	2-1, 1-2	2-2, 4-0	1-4, 1-1	2-2, 0-2
Rangers	1-1, 2-1	2-2, 0-3	2-1, 1-1	2-2, 1-4	2-3, 3-5	3-1, 1-3
St. Mirren	0-2, 2-2	2-1, 3-3	2-1, 2-4	2-0, 1-0	1-1. 2-4	5-5, 3-2
Stirling Albion		1-2, 1-2	4-1, 4-2	6-1, 3-0		
Third Lanark	7-1, 0-2					4-0, 1-1

First Division

	1958-59	1959-60	1960-61	1961-62	1962-63	1963-64
Aberdeen	1-0, 0-4	2-1, 4-6	2-2, 4-1	1-1, 2-1	0-3, 2-3	2-0, 3-1
Airdrie	2-3, 3-4	3-3, 11-1	3-3, 3-4	2-2, 2-4	0-2, 1-2	2-1, 3-5
Arbroath		5-0, 3-2				
Ayr United		5-1, 1-2	3-1, 1-0			
Celtic	3-2, 0-3	3-3, 0-1	0-6, 0-2	1-1, 3-4	1-1, 0-2	1-1, 0-5
Clyde	2-1, 1-4	5-5, 1-2	4-0, 3-3		1-2, 1-3	
Dundee	1-2, 1-2	5-2, 3-6	1-0, 1-0	1-3, 0-1	2-2, 3-1	0-4, 0-3
Dundee United			2-0, 1-3	3-2, 0-4	1-1, 0-5	2-3, 1-1
Dunfermline Ath.	3-1, 2-1	7-4, 2-2	2-1, 2-4	1-2, 0-4	1-1, 2-3	0-0, 0-3
East Stirling						5-2, 3-1
Falkirk	2-3, 0-1			2-2, 4-1	0-3, 1-3	2-2, 4-1
Hearts	0-4, 3-1	1-5, 2-2	1-4, 2-1	1-4, 2-4	0-4, 3-3	1-1, 2-4
Kilmarnock	4-3, 1-1	4-2, 1-3	4-0, 2-3	3-2, 2-4	0-2, 0-2	0-2, 1-2
Motherwell	2-2, 5-2	1-3, 4-3	2-1,1-4	1-2, 1-5	1-0, 2-2	3-1, 3-4
Partick This.	4-0, 2-2	2-2,10-2	1-1, 1-3	3-0, 1-4	0-2, 2-2	2-1, 1-2
Queen of the South	4-0, 4-1				3-0, 4-0	5-2, 2-3
Raith Rovers	4-2, 2-5	0-3, 2-4	0-1, 2-0	3-2, 2-0	1-0, 4-0	
Rangers	2-2, 0-4	0-1, 1-1	1-2, 0-1	0-0, 0-3	1-5, 1-3	0-1, 0-5
St. Johnstone			3-1, 0-2	3-2, 2-0		4-1, 1-0
St. Mirren	0-1, 1-2	1-3, 3-2	4-3, 1-2	2-1, 3-2	2-1, 2-2	1-0, 1-1
Stirlng Albion	0-1, 3-0	3-1, 3-2		3-1, 1-0		
Third Lanark	4-4, 2-2	6-0, 3-5	8-4, 1-6	1-3, 2-1	1-1, 4-1	3-0, 0-1

First Division

	1964-65	1965-66	1966-67	1967-68	1968-69	1969-70
Aberdeen	4-2, 1-1	0-1, 3-1	1-0, 1-2	1-0, 0-5	1-1, 6-2	1-2, 2-0
Airdrie	5-1, 1-0		0-2, 1-0	5-0, 2-1	5-1, 1-3	3-1, 2-3
Arbroath					1-2, 4-3	
Ayr United			2-0, 4-1			4-3, 0-3
Celtic	0-4, 4-2	0-0, 0-2	3-5, 0-2	0-2, 0-4	2-5, 1-1	1-2. 2-1
Clyde	4-3, 3-1	3-1, 2-1	1-1, 1-5	2-1, 2-2	2-1, 1-1	1-0, 0-1
Dundee	2-2, 1-2	1-1, 3-4	2-1, 1-2	2-1. 4-1	1-3, 0-0	4-1, 0-1
Dundee United	3-4, 1-0	3-3, 4-5	2-2, 3-1	3-1, 2-2	1-1, 0-3	3-1, 1-0
Dunfermline Ath.	1-0, 0-1	1-1, 2-3	2-0, 6-5	2-0, 1-0	3-1, 1-1	3-0, 2-1
Falkirk	6-0, 1-0	5-1, 2-3	3-1, 2-0	1-1, 3-2	3-2, 1-0	
Hamilton Acads.		11-1, 2-1				
Hearts	3-5, 1-0	2-3, 4-0	3-1, 0-0	1-0, 4-1	1-3, 0-0	0-0, 2-0
Kilmarnock	1-2, 3-4	3-3, 0-1	3-1, 1-2	3-3, 0-1	1-0, 1-2	2-1, 2-2
Morton	2-1, 2-3	4-1, 5-4		0-1, 0-2	5-0, 3-4	1-0, 1-1
Motherwell	2-0, 2-0	2-2, 0-4	2-1, 2-1	2-1, 1-0		1-1, 1-2
Patick This.	2-1, 2-4	2-0, 2-3	7-0, 4-1	5-1, 2-1	1-2, 1-2	5-1, 1-3
Raith Rovers				3-0, 2-2	3-0, 0-2	3-1, 3-0
Rangers	1-0, 4-2	1-2, 0-2	1-2, 0-1	1-3, 0-2	1-2, 1-6	2-2, 3-1
St. Johnstone	2-0, 3-1	3-0, 3-1	2-5, 2-1	4-2, 3-2	1-2, 4-0	4-1, 0-1
St. MIrren	1-1. 0-0	3-2, 2-0	1-1, 3-1		3-0, 0-3	2-0, 3-3
Stirling Albion		1-0, 2-1	6-0, 0-1	5-2, 1-4		
Third Lanark	5-0, 2-0					

First Division

	1970-71	1971-72	1972-73	1973-74	1974-75
Aberdeen	2-1, 0-3	2-2, 1-2	3-2, 0-1	3-1, 1-1	0-1, 3-2
Airdrie	3-1, 0-2	1-3, 2-2	5-2, 4-0		6-1, 0-0
Arbroath			0-0, 3-2	2-1, 2-3	2-1, 2-0
Ayr United	4-0, 0-2	1-0, 2-1	8-1, 1-1	4-2, 1-1	2-1, 2-2
Celtic	2-0, 1-2	0-1, 1-2	0-3, 1-1	2-4, 1-1	2-1, 0-5
Clyde	5-1, 0-0	1-0, 1-2		5-0, 1-1	1-0, 3-0
Cowdenbeath	2-2, 4-1				
Dumbarton			5-0, 2-2	3-0, 3-3	2-0, 3-2
Dundee	1-2, 0-1	1-0, 2-1	1-1, 0-1	2-1, 3-1	2-1, 0-0
Dundee United	0-1, 1-1	3-0, 4-1	3-1, 0-1	3-1, 4-1	3-0, 3-1
Dunfermline Ath.	2-2, 3-3	2-0, 1-2		1-1, 3-2	5-1, 1-1
East Fife		2-1, 1-2	1-0, 1-0	2-1, 3-0	
Falkirk	1-3, 0-0	6-0, 3-2	3-0, 0-1	2-0, 0-0	
Hearts	0-0, 0-0	0-0, 2-0	2-0, 7-0	3-1, 1-4	2-1, 0-0
Kilmarnock	1-0, 1-4	3-2, 1-1	4-1, 2-2		0-2, 1-1
Morton	2-4, 1-2	1-0, 1-1	2-1, 3-0	5-0, 3-0	5-0, 1-0
Motherwell	1-0, 0-4	1-2, 1-1	0-1, 1-1	1-0, 1-1	6-2, 1-4
Partick This.		3-0, 1-0	2-0, 3-1	2-1, 0-1	2-2, 5-1
Rangers	3-2, 1-1	0-1, 2-1	1-2, 0-1	3-1, 0-4	1-1, 1-0
St. Johnstone	1-2, 1-0	7-1, 2-0	3-2, 3-1	3-3, 2-0	0-1, 2-2
St. Mirren	3-3, 1-3				

Premier League

	1975-76	1976-77	1977-78	1978-79	1979-80
Aberdeen	3-1, 2-2	0-0, 0-1	2-0, 2-1	2-1, 1-4	1-1, 0-3
	3-2, 0-3	0-0, 0-0	1-1, 0-3	1-1, 0-0	0-5, 1-1
Ayr United	1-0, 3-1	1-0, 3-2	1-2, 1-0		
	3-0, 0-2	2-0, 2-1	4-2, 0-2		
Celtic	1-3, 1-1	1-1, 1-1	1-1, 1-3	2-2, 1-0	1-3, 0-3
	2-0, 0-4	0-1, 2-4	4-1, 1-2	2-1, 1-3	1-1, 0-4
Clydebank			2-0, 0-1		
			2-0, 3-0		
Dundee	1-1, 0-2				5-2, 1-2
	4-0, 1-1				2-0, 0-3
Dundee United	1-1, 0-1	1-2, 1-2	0-0, 0-2	1-1, 0-0	0-2, 0-2
	0-1, 0-2	0-0, 0-1	3-1, 1-1	1-0, 1-2	0-2, 0-1
Hearts	1-0, 1-1	1-1, 1-0		1-2, 1-1	
	3-0, 1-0	3-1, 2-2		1-1, 2-1	
Kilmarnock		2-0, 1-1			1-1, 0-1
		0-0, 1-0			1-2, 1-3
Morton				1-1, 2-2	1-1, 0-2
				1-1, 0-3	3-2, 1-1
Motherwell	1-0, 1-2	0-2, 2-2	0-0, 0-1	2-2, 3-2	
	2-0, 1-0	1-2, 1-1	2-1, 4-2	4-0, 3-0	
Partick This.		0-0, 1-1	2-3, 0-1	0-0, 1-2	2-1, 1-2
		1-1, 0-1	3-1, 1-2	1-0, 1-6	0-1, 0-1
Rangers	2-1, 1-1	1-1, 1-1	0-1, 2-0	0-0, 1-2	1-3, 0-2
	0-3, 0-2	0-0, 1-2	1-1, 0-0	2-1, 0-1	2-1, 0-1
St. Johnstone	4-2, 4-3				
	5-0, 2-0				
St. Mirren			2-0, 0-3	1-0, 0-1	0-2, 1-2
			5-1, 0-3	0-2, 3-2	2-1, 0-2

First Division
1980-81

Ayr United	1-0, 3-1 1-0	Falkirk	2-0, 2-0 1-0
Berwick Rangers	3-0, 2-0 0-0	Hamilton Acads.	3-3, 1-1 4-0
Clydebank	4-1, 1-1 3-0	Motherwell	1-0, 0-2 1-1
Dunfermline Ath.	1-0, 2-0 5-0	Raith Rovers	0-1, 0-2 2-0
Dumbarton	1-0, 0-2 4-1	St. Johnstone	4-0, 2-1 1-2
Dundee	0-0, 2-1 0-1	Stirling Albion	3-0, 2-0 0-0
E. Stirlingshire	2-2, 1-1 2-0		

All the Facts

Premier League

	1981-82	1982-83	1983-84	1984-85	1985-86
Aberdeen	1-1, 0-1 0-3, 1-3	1-1, 0-2 0-0, 0-5	2-1, 1-2 0-2, 2-2	0-3, 1-4 0-5, 0-2	1-1, 0-3 0-1, 0-4
Airdrieonains	1-1, 1-3 1-0, 2-0				
Celtic	1-0, 0-0 1-0, 0-6	2-3, 0-2 0-3, 1-4	0-2, 1-5 0-1, 2-3	0-0, 0-3 0-1, 1-0	0-5, 1-1 2-2, 0-2
Clydebank					5-0, 4-2 2-3, 3-1
Dumbarton				2-3, 2-2 3-1, 2-0	
Dundee	2-0, 0-0 2-1, 2-2	1-1, 1-2 0-0, 1-0	2-1, 3-0 3-1, 2-1	2-0, 1-0 0-1, 0-2	2-1, 0-1 1-0, 1-3
Dundee United	1-1, 0-1 0-1, 1-0	0-0, 0-3 0-0, 3-3	0-2, 0-5 1-0, 0-2	0-0, 1-2 1-1, 0-2	0-1, 2-2 1-2, 0-4
Hearts			1-1, 2-3 0-0, 1-1	1-2, 0-0 1-2, 2-2	0-0, 1-2 1-2, 1-3
Kilmarnock		2-2, 1-1 8-1, 2-0			
Morton	4-0, 1-2 2-2, 0-0	1-2, 0-0 2-0, 1-0		3-1, 0-4 5-1, 2-1	
Motherwell		1-0, 1-0 1-1, 0-2	2-1, 2-1 1-2, 3-2		1-0, 0-2 4-0, 1-3
Partick This.	3-0, 0-1 1-1, 2-1				
Rangers	1-2, 2-2 0-0, 1-1	0-0, 2-3 1-2, 1-1	0-2, 0-1 0-0, 0-0	2-2, 0-2 1-2, 2-1	1-3, 2-1 1-1, 1-3
St. Johnstone			4-1, 3-0 1-2, 0-1		
St. Mirren	0-0, 0-1 2-1, 2-2	0-0, 0-3 1-1, 0-3	3-1, 1-2 1-1, 1-3	2-3, 0-2 0-4, 1-2	2-3, 3-1 3-0, 2-0

Premier League

	1986-87	1987-88	1988-89	1989-90
Aberdeen	1-1, 0-4	0-2, 1-1	1-2, 0-0	0-3, 0-1
	1-1, 0-1	0-0, 2-0	1-2, 0-2	3-2, 2-1
Celtic	0-1, 1-5	0-1, 1-1	3-1, 0-1	0-3, 1-3
	1-4, 0-1	0-2, 0-2	1-3, 0-1	1-0, 1-1
Clydebank	3-2, 0-0			
	4-1, 2-1			
Dundee	0-3, 0-3	0-4, 1-2	1-1, 1-2	3-2, 0-0
	2-2, 0-2	2-1, 0-0	1-1, 2-1	1-1, 0-2
Dundee United	1-1, 0-1	0-1, 2-1	1-1, 1-1	2-0, 0-1
	0-2, 1-2	0-0, 2-1	1-2, 1-4	0-0, 0-1
Dunfermline Ath.		4-0, 3-3		2-2, 0-0
		2-0, 0-1		2-1, 1-1
Falkirk	1-0, 1-1	1-0, 1-1		
	2-0, 3-1	0-0, 0-1		
Hamilton Acads.	1-3, 4-1		1-0, 3-0	
	1-1, 1-0		2-1, 3-0	
Hearts	1-3, 1-1	2-1, 0-1	0-0, 2-1	1-1, 0-1
	2-2, 1-2	0-0, 0-0	1-0, 1-3	1-2, 0-2
Morton		0-0, 3-3		
		3-1, 1-1		
Motherwell	0-0, 1-4	1-0, 0-1	1-0, 1-1	3-2, 2-0
	0-1, 1-2	1-1, 2-0	2-0, 0-0	1-2, 0-1
Rangers	2-1, 0-3	1-0, 0-1	0-1, 0-0	2-0, 0-3
	0-0, 1-1	0-2, 1-1	0-1, 0-1	0-0, 1-0
St. Mirren	0-1, 1-3	1-1, 2-2	2-0, 2-0	2-1, 0-0
	1-0, 1-1	0-0, 1-1	1-0, 1-3	0-1, 1-0

European Record

Season	Tournament		Opponents	Ven	Score	Tie-break
1955–56	European	1	Rot-Weiss Essen (WG)	a	4-0, 1-1	
		2	Djurgaarden (SWE)	a	3-1, 1-0	
		S	Stade Reim (FR)	a	0-2, 0-1	
1960–61	Fairs	1	Lausanne Sports (SWZ)	a	w. o.	
		2	Barcelona (SP)	a	4-4, 3-2	
		S	Roma (IT)	h	2-2, 3-3, 0-6 (a)	
1961–62	Fairs	1	Belenenses (POR)	h	3-3, 3-1	
		2	Red Star Belgrade (YUG)	a	0-4, 0-1	
1962–63	Fairs	1	Staevnet Copenhagen (DEN)	h	4-0, 3-2	
		2	Utrecht (HOL)	h	2-1, 1-0	
		3	Valencia (SP)	a	0-5, 2-1	
1965–66	Fairs	1	Valencia (SP)	h	2-0, 0-2, 0-3 (a)	
1967–68	Fairs	1	Porto (POR)	h	3-0, 1-3	
		2	Napoli (IT)	a	1-4, 5-0	
		3	Leeds United (ENG)	a	0-1, 1-1	
1968–69	Fairs	1	Olympia Ljubjana (YUG)	a	3-0, 2-1	
		2	Lokomotive Leipzig (EG)	h	3-1, 1-0	
		3	Hamburg (WG)	a	0-1, 2-1, away goals	
1970–71	Fairs	1	Malmoe (SWE)	h	6-0, 3-2	
		2	Virotia Guimares (POR)	h	2-0, 1-2	
		3	Liverpool (ENG)	h	0-1, 0-2	
1972–73	Cup Win.	1	Sporting Lisbon (POR)	a	1-2, 6-1	
		2	Besa (ALB)	h	7-1, 1-1	
		3	Hajduk Split (YUG)	h	4-2, 0-3	
1973–74	Fairs	1	Keflavik (ICE)	h	2-0, 1-1	
		2	Leeds United (ENG)	a	0-0, 0-0, penalties (lost)	
1974–75	UEFA	1	Rosenborg Trondheim (NOR)	a	3-2, 9-1	
		2	Juventus (IT)	h	2-4, 0-4	
1975–76	UEFA	1	Liverpool (ENG)	h	1-0, 1-3	
1976–77	UEFA	1	Sochaux (FR)	h	1-0, 0-0	
		2	Oesters Vaxjoe (SWE)	h	2-0, 1-4	
1978–79	UEFA	1	Norrkoping (SWE)	h	3-2, 0-0	
		2	Racing Strasbourg (FR)	a	0-2, 1-0	
1989–90	UEFA	1	Videoton (HUN)	h	1-0, 3-0	
		2	Royal Liège (BEL)	h	0-0, 0-1 aet	

League Cup Record

1946–47 :	Section	v. Celtic	4-2, 1-1
		v. Hamilton Acads.	2-0, 6-3
		v. Third Lanark	1-2, 2-1
		v. Airdrie (a)	4-4, 1-0 *aet*
		v. Rangers (n)	1-3
1947–48 :	Section	v. Airdrie	5-0, 1-1
		v. Clyde	5-1, 4-3
		v. Hearts	1-2, 1-2
1948–49 :	Section	v. Celtic	4-2, 0-1
		v. Clyde	4-0, 4-1
		v. Rangers	0-0, 0-1
1949–50 :	Section	v. Falkirk	1-0, 1-2
		v. Queen of the South	5-3, 2-1
		v. Third Lanark	4-2, 2-0
	QF	v. Partick Thistle (a)	2-4, 4-0
	SF	v. Dunfermline Ath. (n)	1-2
1950–51 :	Section	v. Dundee	2-0, 2-0 *(abandoned)*
		v. Falkirk	4-0, 5-4
		v. St. Mirren	5-0, 6-0
	QF	v. Aberdeen (a)	1-4, 4-1, 1-1, 5-1
	SF	v. Queen of the South (n)	3-1
	F	v. Motherwell (n)	0-3
1951–52 :	Section	v. Motherwell	0-4, 0-1
		v. Partick Thistle	5-1, 2-4
		v. Stirling Albion	4-2, 1-1
1952–53 :	Section	v. Celtic	3-0, 0-1
		v. Partick Thistle	3-1, 5-1
		v. St. Mirren	5-2, 1-3
	QF	v. Morton (a)	6-0, 6-3
	SF	v. Dundee (n)	1-2
1953–54 :	Section	v. Falkirk	4-1, 2-1
		v. Queen of the South	2-1, 4-0
		v. St. Mirren	3-2, 2-2
	QF	v. Third Lanark (a)	4-0, 4-0
	SF	v. East Fife (n)	2-3
1954–55 :	Section	v. Aberdeen	2-0, 1-1
		v. East Fife	1-2, 1-3
		v. Queen of the South	3-1, 5-3

1955–56	:	Section	v. Aberdeen	0-1, 1-2
			v. Clyde	2-1, 2-2
			v. Dunfemline Ath.	3-1, 3-1
1956–57	:	Section	v. Falkirk	0-1, 0-4
			v. Hearts	1-2, 1-6
			v. Partick Thistle	2-2, 1-4
1957–58	:	Section	v. Airdrie	5-1, 1-4
			v. Celtic	3-1, 0-2
			v. East Fife	4-0, 2-2
1958–59	:	Section	v. Aberdeen	4-2, 2-1
			v. Falkirk	3-2, 4-0
			v. Kilmarnock	0-3, 1-2
1959–60	:	Section	v. Dundee	1-3, 3-4
			v. Motherwell	1-3, 2-4
			v. Rangers	1-6, 1-5
1960–61	:	Section	v. Airdrie	6-1, 1-3
			v. Dunfermline Ath.	3-0, 1-3
			v. Kilmarnock	2-2, 2-4
1961–62	:	Section	v. Celtic	2-2, 1-2
			v. Partick Thistle	2-1, 1-2
			v. St. Johnstone	4-1, 1-1
1962–63	:	Section	v. Rangers	1-4, 0-0
			v. St. Mirren	2-0, 3-3
			v. Third Lanark	3-2, 4-1
1963–64	:	Section	v. Aberdeen	2-2, 2-0
			v. Dundee United	3-2, 4-2
			v. St. Mirren	3-0, 1-1
		QF	v. Dundee (a)	3-3, 2-0
		SF	v. Morton (a)	1-1, 0-1
1964–65	:	Section	v. Airdrie	5-0, 4-1
			v. Dunfermline Ath.	1-1, 0-2
			v. Third Lanark	3-0, 2-0
1965–66	:	Section	v. Falkirk	3-1, 1-3
			v. Morton	3-0, 4-2
			v. St. Mirren	1-0, 3-0
		QF	v. Alloa Ath (a)	2-0, 11-2
		SF	v. Celtic (n)	2-2, 0-4
1966–67	:	Section	v. Kimarnock	2-1, 0-3
			v. Rangers	3-2, 0-1
			v. Stirling Albion	3-0, 4-2

1967–68 :	Section	v. Clyde	3-1, 2-0
		v. Dundee	2-4, 0-0
		v. Motherwell	1-0, 1-2
1968–69 :	Section	v. Falkirk	2-0, 2-0
		v. Raith Rovers	3-0, 1-0
		v. St. Johnstone	0-1, 2-2
	QF	v. East Fife (a)	4-1, 2-1
	SF	v. Dundee (n)	2-1
	F	v. Celtic (n)	2-6
1969–70 :	Section	v. Aberdeen	0-0, 2-2
		v. Clyde	4-1, 1-3
		v. Dunfermline Ath.	2-0, 1-3
1970–71 :	Section	v. Aberdeen	4-0, 1-1
		v. Airdrie	3-2, 4-2
		v. St. Johnstone	1-1, 3-1
	QF	v. Rangers (h)	1-3, 1-3
1971–72 :	Section	v. Dundee United	2-0, 4-1
		v. Kilmarnock	3-1, 0-0
		v. Motherwell	2-1, 3-0
	QF	v. Falkirk (a)	0-2, 1-0
1972–73 :	Section	v. Aberdeen	2-1, 1-4
		v. Queen of the South	3-0, 3-1
		v. Queens Park	4-2, 1-0
	Rd. 2	v. Dundee United (a)	5-2, 0-0
	QF	v. Airdrie (a)	6-2, 4-1
	SF	v. Rangers (n)	1-0
	F	v. Celtic (n)	2-1
1973–74 :	Section	v. Ayr United	1-0, 2-0
		v. Dumbarton	1-0, 1-4
		v. Morton	2-1, 4-1
	Rd. 2	v. Raith Rovers (h)	3-2, 2-0
	QF	v. Rangers (a)	0-2, 0-0
1974–75 :	Section	v. Dundee	4-2, 1-2
		v. Rangers	3-1, 1-0
		v. St. Johnstone	4-0, 3-1
	QF	v. Kilmarnock (a)	3-3, 4-1
	SF	v. Falkirk (n)	1-0
	F	v. Celtic (n)	3-6
1975–76 :	Section	v. Ayr United	2-1, 1-2
		v. Dundee	2-0, 2-1
		v. Dunfermline Ath	3-0, 4-0
	QF	v. Montrose (h)	1-0, 1-3 *aet*

1976–77 :	Section	v. Montrose	0-0, 1-0	
		v. Rangers	1-1, 0-3	
		v. St. Johnstone	9-2, 2-1	
1977–78 :	Rd. 1	bye		
	Rd. 2	v. Queen of the South (h)	1-2, 0-0	
1978–79 :	Rd. 1	bye		
	Rd. 2	v. Brechin City (a)	3-0, 3-1	
	Rd. 3	v. Clydebank (h)	1-0, 1-1	
	Rd. 4	v. Morton (a)	0-1, 2-0	
	SF	v. Aberdeen (n)	0-1	aet
1979–80 :	Rd. 1	bye		
	Rd. 2	v. Montrose (h)	2-1, 1-1	
	Rd. 3	v. Kilmarnock (h)	1-2, 1-2	
1980–81 :	Rd. 1	bye		
	Rd. 2	v. Alloa Athletic (a)	2-0, 1-1	
	Rd. 3	v. Clyde (a)	2-0, 2-1	
	Rd. 4	v. Ayr United (a)	2-2, 0-2	aet
1981–82 :	Section	v. Celtic	1-4, 1-4	
		v. St. Johnstone	1-2, 2-1	
		v. St. Mirren	0-1, 0-0	
1982–83 :	Section	v. Airdrie	1-1, 1-3	
		v. Clydebank	1-1, 2-0	
		v. Rangers	1-1, 0-0	
1983–84 :	Rd. 1	bye		
	Rd. 2	v. Dumbarton (h)	5-0, 2-1	
	Section	v. Airdrie	0-0, 3-1	
		v. Celtic	0-0, 1-5	
		v. Kilmarnock	2-0, 1-3	
1984–85 :	Rd. 1	bye		
	Rd. 2	v. East Fife (h)	1-0	
	Rd. 3	v. Meadowbank Thistle (h)	1-2	aet
1985–86	Rd. 2	v. Cowdenbeath (h)	6-0	
	Rd. 3	v. Motherwell (h)	6-1	
	Rd. 4	v. Celtic (h)	4-4; won pens	
	S	v. Rangers (h)	2-0, 0-1	
	F	v. Aberdeen	0-3	
1986–87	Rd. 2	v. East Stirlingshire (h)	1-0	
	Rd. 3	v. Hamilton Acads (a)	1-0	
	Rd. 4	v. Dundee United (h)	0-2	

1987–88	Rd. 2	v.	Montrose (h)	3-2
	Rd. 3	v.	Queen of the South (h)	3-1
	Rd. 4	v.	Motherwell (a)	0-1
1988–89	Rd. 2	v.	Stranraer (h)	4-0
	Rd. 3	v.	Kilmarnock (h)	1-0
	Rd. 4	v.	Aberdeen (h)	1-2 *aet*
1989–90	Rd. 2	v.	Alloa Athletic (h)	2-0
	Rd. 3	v.	Clydebank (h)	0-0; *won pens*
	Rd. 4	v.	Dunfermline Ath	1-3 *aet*

Rosebery Charity Cup Record

1882–83	SF	v.	Hearts (a)	1-3
1883–84	SF	v.	University (n)	5-0
	F	v.	St. Bernards	1-1, 1-0
1884–85	SF	v.	St. Bernards (a)	4-0
	F	v.	Hearts (n)	3-0
1885–86	SF	v.	University (n)	3-1
	F	v.	Hearts (a)	*2-0, *0-2, 0-1

*: Result protested

1886–87	SF	v.	St. Bernards (a)	2-2, 2-2, 6-1
	F	v.	Hearts (n)	7-1
1887–88	SF	v.	Hearts (n)	6-0
	F	v.	Mossend Swifts (n)	1-0
1888–89	*Hibs did not take part*			
1889–90	SF	v.	Hearts (n)	2-3
1890–91	*Hibs did not take part*			
1891–92	*Hibs did not take part*			
1892–93	*Hibs did not take part*			
1893–94	SF	v.	St. Bernards (n)	2-1
	F	v.	Hearts (n)	4-2
1894–95	SF	v.	Leith Athletic (n)	1-1

Leith awarded tie when Hibs refused to play extra time

1895–96	SF	v.	Hearts (n)	0-2
1896–97	SF	v.	Leith Athletic (n)	7-0
	F	v.	Hearts (n)	3-0
1897–98	SF	v.	St. Bernards (n)	1-1, 4-1
	F	v.	Hearts (n)	1-6
1898–99	SF	v.	Hearts (n)	2-3
1899–1900	SF	v.	Leith Athletic (h)	3-2
	F	v.	Hearts (a)	3-3, 0-3
1900–01	SF	v.	Leith Athletic (h)	3-0
	F	v.	Hearts (a)	4-0
1901–02	SF	v.	Leith Athletic (h)	4-2
	F	v.	Hearts (h)	1-0
1902–03	SF	v.	St. Bernards (a)	2-1
	F	v.	Leith Athletic (h)	3-1
1903–04	SF	v.	St. Bernards (n)	2-0
	F	v.	Hearts (a)	0-3

1904–05	SF	v.	Leith Athletic (h)	0-3
1905–06	SF	v.	Leith (h)	3-2
	F	v.	Hearts (a)	2-0
1906–07	SF	v.	Hearts (a)	0-1
1907–08	SF	v.	St. Bernards (n)	1-1
	St. Bernards won on corners			
1908–09	SF	v.	Hearts (h)	2-1
	F	v.	Leith (h)	3-0
1909–10	SF	v.	Hearts (a)	1-0
	F	v.	Leith (h)	2-0
1910–11	SF	v.	Hearts (a)	2-1
	F	v.	St. Bernards (h)	5-0
1911–12	SF	v.	St. Bernards (h)	2-0
	F	v.	Rest of Edinburgh (h)	0-0
	Hibs won on corners			
1912–13	SF	v.	Leith (a)	1-0
	F	v.	Hearts (a)	2-0
1913–14	SF	v.	Leith (h)	6-1
	F	v.	Hearts (h)	2-3
1914–15	SF	v.	Leith (a)	4-1
	F	v.	St. Bernards (n)	3-4
1915–16	SF	v.	St. Bernards (h)	6-1
	F	v.	Hearts (a)	0-4
1916–17	F	v.	Hearts (a)	0-3
1917–18	*No competition*			
1918–19	SF	v.	Hearts (a)	1-2
1919–20	SF	v.	Armadale (h)	3-2
	F	v.	Hearts (a)	0-2
1920–21	SF	v.	St. Bernards (h)	1-3
1921–22	SF	v.	Hearts (a)	1-0
	F	v.	Leith Athletic (n)	3-0
1922–23	SF	v.	Leith Athletic (h)	6-1
	F	v.	Hearts (a)	1-2
1923–24	SF	v.	St. Bernards (n)	2-1
	F	v.	Hearts (a)	2-0
1924–25	SF	v.	Leith Athletic (h)	4-0
	F	v.	Hearts (a)	1-0
1925–26	SF	v.	Leith Athletic (h)	1-4

1926–27	SF	v.	St. Bernards (h)	5-1
	F	v.	Hearts (a)	0-1
1927–28	SF	v.	Leith Athletic (h)	1-3
1928–29	SF	v.	St. Bernards (h)	2-1
	F	v.	Hearts (a)	1-5
1929–30	SF	v.	Leith Athletic (h)	0-2
1930–31	SF	v.	St. Bernards (h)	1-3
1931–32	SF	v.	Leith Athletic (h)	3-4
1932–33	SF	v.	Motherwell (h)	0-1
1933–34	QF	v.	St. Bernards (h)	1-0
	SF	v.	St. Johnstone (h)	2-1
	F	v.	Hearts (a)	0-2
1934–35	QF	v.	Dunfermline Ath. (h)	2-3
1935–36	SF	v.	St. Bernards (h)	2-3
1936–37	SF	v.	Leith Athletic (h)	3-1
	F	v.	Hearts (a)	0-2
1937–38	SF	v.	St. Bernards (h)	0-1
1938–39	SF	v.	Leith Athletic (h)	1-2
1939–40	SF	v.	St. Bernards (h)	4-2
	F	v.	Hearts (a)	5-2
1940–41	F	v.	Hearts (h)	0-2
1941–42	F	v.	Hearts (a)	1-1
1942–43	F	v.	Hearts (h)	1-1

Hearts won on toss of coin

| 1943–44 | F | v. | Hearts (a) | 4-1 |
| 1944–45 | F | v. | Hearts (h) | 1-1 |

Hibs won on corners

Wartime Competitions – 1939-46

First Division

	1939–40
Aberdeen	1-3
Albion Rovers	3-5
Clyde	3-2
Queen of the South	3-1, 1-2

Regional League – East Div.

	1939–40
Aberdeen	2-0, 3-3
Alloa Athletic	3-0, 3-2
Arbroath	2-4, 0-0
Cowdenbeath	4-0
Dundee	6-0, 1-2
Dundee United	6-2, 3-1
Dunfermline Ath.	2-3, 1-2
Falkirk	5-6, 3-3
Hearts	5-6, 0-4
Kings Park	2-1, 7-2
Raith Rovers	4-1, 1-1
St. Bernards	3-1, 6-1
St. Johnstone	3-3, 0-4
Stenhousemuir	1-2, 1-2

Emergency War Cup – 1940

Rd. 1	v.	Falkirk (a)	0-5, 4-0

Summer Cup

1941

Rd. 1	v.	Celtic (a)	5-2, 0-1
2	v.	Clyde (h)	1-2, 4-3, 2-1
S	v.	Dumbarton (n)	1-0
F	v.	Rangers (n)	3-2

1942

Rd. 1	v.	Clyde (h)	2-1, 2-0
2	v.	Third Lanark (h)	8-2, 5-1
S	v.	Motherwell (n)	3-1
F	v.	Rangers (n)	0-0

Rangers won by toss of coin

1943

Rd. 1	v.	Partick Thistle (h)	7-0, 5-2
2	v.	Queens Park (a)	2-1, 4-0
S	v.	Rangers (n)	1-3

1944

Rd. 1	v.	Airdrie (a)	4-2, 3-0
2	v.	Morton (a)	1-1, 0-2

1945

Rd. 1	v.	St. Mirren (a)	2-4, 7-0
2	v.	Falkirk (h)	3-1, 0-1
S	v.	Celtic (n)	2-0
F	v.	Partick Thistle (n)	0-2

Victory Cup 1946

Rd. 1	v.	Dundee (h)	3-0, 0-2
2	v.	Hearts (h)	3-1
3	v.	Partick Thistle (a)	1-1, 2-0
S	v.	Clyde (n)	2-1
F	v.	Rangers (n)	1-3

Southern League

	1940–41	1941–42	1942–43	1943–44	1944–45	1945–46
Aberdeen						1-1, 1-2
Airdrie	2-2, 2-4	4-1, 2-1	7-1, 5-0	1-2, 5-2	3-2, 1-1	
Albion Rovers	1-1, 3-4	5-2, 8-3	3-1, 4-1	3-0, 4-2	4-1, 5-0	
Celtic	2-0, 4-0	1-3, 1-2	4-0, 3-0	2-2, 2-2	2-4, 1-1	1-1, 1-0
Clyde	2-2, 1-2	1-4, 3-2	2-2, 2-7	3-1, 1-2	0-4, 3-2	3-2, 2-2
Dumbarton	3-1, 0-2	4-0, 1-2	4-1, 4-1	4-3, 1-1	0-0, 3-0	
Falkirk	7-1, 2-2	2-0, 2-1	4-0, 1-3	4-3, 5-3	3-0, 3-1	4-1, 1-2
Hamilton Acads.	3-1, 3-2	4-0, 2-2	3-1, 3-1	3-5, 2-1	3-1, 1-1	1-2, 1-1
Hearts	2-1, 5-3	2-2, 4-2	2-2, 4-1	0-1, 1-0	3-1, 0-3	1-0, 2-0
Kilmarnock						4-1, 4-3
Morton	2-1, 1-3	1-0, 1-2	2-2, 0-1	2-0, 1-3	0-1, 2-3	5-0, 1-4
Motherwell	3-3, 0-3	3-1, 2-3	2-1, 1-2	3-3, 1-0	0-1, 0-3	0-0, 0-0
Partick Thistle	4-0, 2-1	4-0, 2-3	0-0, 5-1	2-0, 1-3	8-0, 1-5	3-1, 2-0
Queen of the South						6-1, 0-3
Queens Park	3-2, 5-2	1-1, 2-1	4-0, 3-2	2-1, 2-4	2-0, 2-0	4-0, 4-2
Rangers	1-0, 1-5	8-1, 1-0	1-1, 1-1	3-4, 0-4	4-1, 0-5	2-1, 2-3
St. Mirren	2-4, 4-4	5-2, 1-1	3-2, 2-1	4-1, 2-1	6-2, 1-1	3-2, 3-0
Third Lanark	2-2, 2-3	6-0, 2-4	5-1, 2-3	6-0, 2-0	2-4, 6-3	4-0, 1-2

Southern League Cup

1940–41

Sec.	v.	Clyde	5-4, 4-2
	v.	Hearts	3-2, 2-5
	v.	Queens Park	0-0, 1-2

1941–42

Sec.	v.	Hamilton Acads.	1-2, 1-3
	v.	Celtic	1-0, 2-4
	v.	Queens Park	3-1, 1-0

1942–43

Sec.	v.	Celtic	2-1, 1-2
	v.	St. Mirren	2-1, 3-1
	v.	Rangers	0-2, 0-1

1943–44

Sec.	v.	Third Lanark	4-0, 4-0
	v.	Albion Rovers	2-1, 1-0
	v.	Morton	6-3, 2-2
S	v.	Clyde (n)	5-2
F	v.	Rangers (n)	0-0

Hibs won by 6 cnrs to 5

1944–45

Sec.	v.	Third Lanark	3-1, 1-2
	v.	Rangers	1-1, 0-2
	v.	Albion Rovers	1-1, 8-1

1945–46

Sec.	v.	Partick Thistle	1-0, 1-0
	v.	Aberdeen	3-2, 1-4
	v.	Kilmarnock	4-0, 0-1

Other Competitions

President's Trophy (1879)

Rd.	1	v.	Brunswick	6-0
	2	v.	Thistle	0-0, 3-1
	SF	v.	Hearts	0-1

Glasgow Charity Cup (1887)

Rd.	1	v.	Renton (n)	2-3

Glasgow Charity Cup (1888)

Rd.	1	v.	Cambuslang (n)	0-3

Glasgow Charity Cup (1902)

Rd.	1	v.	Rangers (n)	1-0
	SF	v.	St. Mirren (n)	3-0
	F	v.	Celtic (n)	6-2

Glasgow Charity Cup (1903)

Rd.	1	v.	Celtic (n)	0-0, 0-5

Victory Cup (1919)

Rd.	1	v.	bye	
	2	v.	Ayr United (h)	1-0
	3	v.	Motherwell (h)	2-0
	SF	v.	St. Mirren (n)	1-3 aet

St. Mungo's Cup (1951)

Rd.	1	v.	Third Lanark (h)	3-1
	2	v.	Motherwell (n)	3-1
	SF	v.	Aberdeen (n)	1-1, 1-2

Coronation Cup (1953)

Rd.	1	v.	Tottenham Hotspur (n)	1-1, 2-1
	SF	v.	Newcastle United (n)	4-0
	F	v.	Celtic (n)	0-2

Summer Cup (1964)

Section	v.	Hearts	1-0, 2-3
	v.	Dunfermline Ath.	1-1, 1-1
	v.	Falkirk	4-0, 2-4
Play-off	v.	Dunfermline Ath (n)	3-1
Semi-final	v.	Kilmarnock (a)	3-4, 3-0
Final	v.	Aberdeen (a)	2-3, 2-1, 3-1

Summer Cup (1965)

Section	v.	Hearts	3-0, 2-2
	v.	Dunfermline Ath.	1-2, 2-1
	v.	Falkirk	3-2, 3-1
Semi-final	v.	Motherwell (h)	2-0, 2-6 aet

Drybrough Cup (1972)

Rd.	1	v. Montrose (h)	4-0
	SF	v. Rangers (h)	3-0
	F	v. Celtic (n)	5-3 aet

Drybrough Cup (1973)

Rd.	1	v. St. Mirren (h)	2-1
	SF	v. Rangers (h)	2-1
	F	v. Celtic (n)	1-0 aet

Drybrough Cup (1974)

Rd.	1	v. Kilmarnock (h)	2-1
	SF	v. Rangers (h)	2-3

Anglo-Scottish Cup (1977–78)

Rd.	1	v. Ayr United (h)	2-1, 2-2
	2	v. Blackburn Rovers (h)	2-1, 1-0
	3	v. Bristol City (h)	1-1, 3-5

Anglo-Scottish Cup (1979–80)

Rd.	1	v. St. Miren (a)	3-3, 0-1

Skol Festival Trophy (1979)

Round Robin ;	v. Hearts (h)	2-1
	v. Manchester City (n)	1-1
	v. Coventry City (n)	0-0

Edinburgh Cup/East of Scotland Shield Record

1875–76	*Hibs did not take part*			
1876–77	Rd.	1	v. Thistle	1-2
1877–78	Rd.	1	v. Hanover	3-1
		S	v. Thistle	4-0
		F	v. Hearts	0-0, 1-1, 1-1, 1-1, 2-3
1878–79	Rd.	1	v. Bellevue	13-0
		2	v. Waverley	7-0
		S	v. Brunswick (h)	6-1
		F	v. Hearts (n)	1-1, 2-0
1879–80	Rd.	1	v. Bellevue (h)	10-1
		2	v. St. Bernards (h)	3-1
		3	v. Brunswick (h)	4-3
		S	v. Hearts (a)	5-2
		F	v. Dunfermline (n)	* 6-3, 5-0

*: result protested

1880–81	Rd.	1	v. Caledonian (h)	11-1
		2	v. Bruntisland This. (h)	15-0
		3	v. Hearts (a)	2-1
		4	v. Rovers (h)	9-0
		S	v. University (a)	5-1
		F	v. St. Bernards (n)	4-4, 1-0
1881–82	Rd.	1	v. Hearts (a)	4-2
		2	v. bye	
		3	v. Kinleith	5-0
		4	v. Hanover (h)	6-1
		S	v. West Calder (h)	7-1
		F	v. St. Bernards (n)	4-2
1882–83	Rd.	1	v. Glencairn (h)	6-1
		2	v. Avondale (h)	8-0
		3	v. Edina (h)	6-0
		4	v. Rose (h)	7-1
		S	v. bye	
		F	v. University	scr.
1883–84	Rd.	1	v. Norton Park (h)	4-1
		2	v. Muirhouse Rovers (h)	11-0
		3	v. Glencairn (h)	5-0
		4	v. East Linton (h)	10-0
		S	v. Hearts (h)	3-1
		F	v. St. Bernards (n)	7-0

Footnote: The Edinburgh Cup was replaced by the East of Scotland Shield when Hibs won the former outright in 1881.

1884–85	Rd. 1	v.	Lorne Star (h)	5-1
	2	v.	Rose (h)	10-0
	3	v.	Sarsfield (h)	10-0
	4	v.	Hearts (h)	3-1
	S	v.	Edinburgh Emmet (h)	20-1
	F	v.	University (n)	3-2
1885–86	Rd. 1	v.	Edina (h)	9-0
	2	v.	Vale of Midlothian (a)	6-0
	3	v.	Mossend Swifts (h)	13-4
	4	v.	Hearts (h)	4-3
	S	v.	University (h)	3-0
	F	v.	St. Bernards (n)	4-1
1886–87	Rd. 1	v.	Vale of Midlothian (h)	4-0
	2	v.	Haddington Rangers	w.o.
	3	v.	Bo'ness (a)	3-1
	4	v.	West Calder (a)	3-1
	S	v.	St. Bernards (h)	4-2
	F	v.	Hearts (n)	3-0
1887–88	Rd. 1	v.	Polton Vale (a)	8-0
	2	v.	University (a)	5-1
	3	v.	Leith Harp (h)	8-1
	S	v.	Hearts (h)	5-2
	F	v.	Mossend Swifts (n)	0-1
1888–89	Rd. 1	v.	Leith Sthletic (a)	2-3
1889–90	Rd. 1	v.	Bonnyrigg Rose (h)	7-1
	2	v.	Cameron Highlanders (h)	5-2
	3	v.	Leith Athletic (h)	2-3
1890–91	Rd. 1	v.	Lassodie (h)	7-1
	2	v.	Hearts (a)	1-2
1891–92	*Hibs did not take part*			
1892–93	*Hibs did not take part*			
1893–94	Rd. Q	v.	Hearts	*4-3, 2-2, 2-3
	: result protested			
1894–95	*Hibs did not take part*			
1895–96	*Hibs did not take part*			
1896–97	*Hibs did not take part*			
1897–98	Rd. Q	v.	Leith Ath (n)	1-2
1898–99	Rd. Q	v.	West Calder (h)	3-2
	S	v.	Leith Ath (a)	10-1
	F	v.	Hearts (n)	0-1

1899–1900	Rd. Q	v.	Mossend Swifts (h)	3-0
	S	v.	St. Bernards (h)	2-2, 2-0
	F	v.	Hearts (h)	3-0
1900–01	Rd. Q	v.	Hearts (h)	1-1, 0-1
1901–02	Rd. Q	v.	Raith Rovers (h)	6-0
	S	v.	St. Bernards (h)	3-0
	F	v.	Hearts (h)	1-2
1902–03	Rd. Q	v.	Cowdenbeath (a)	3-3, 2-0
	S	v.	Broxburn (h)	5-1
	F	v.	Leith Athletic (h)	4-3
1903–04	Rd. S	v.	St. Bernards (a)	0-0

Hibs refused to play extra time

| 1904–05 | Rd. S | v. | St. Bernards | *1-2, 0-0, 1-1, 3-1 |
| | F | v. | Hearts (h) | 1-1, 2-2, 1-0 |

*: result protested

1905–06	Rd. S	v.	Leith Athletic (h)	2-0
	F	v.	Hearts (a)	0-0, 1-2
1906–07	Rd. S	v.	Leith (a)	0-1
1907–08	Rd. S	v.	Hearts (h)	1-1, 1-0
	F	v.	Leith (h)	2-1
1908–09	Rd. S	v.	Leith (h)	2-0
	F	v.	Hearts (h)	2-2, 1-1, 1-0
1909–10	Rd. S	v.	St. Bernards (h)	0-0

abandoned; Hibs scratched

1910–11	Rd. S	v.	St. Bernards (h)	1-0
	F	v.	Leith (h)	0-0, 3-0
1911–12	Rd. S	v.	Leith (h)	4-0
	F	v.	St. Bernards (n)	2-0
1912–13	Rd. S	v.	Hearts (h)	1-1

Hearts scratched

	F	v.	St. Bernards (h)	3-2
1913–14	Rd. S	v.	Hearts (h)	0-1
1914–15	Rd. S	v.	St. Bernards (a)	2-0
	F	v.	Hearts (a)	0-1
1915–17	*No competition*
1917–18	Rd. F	v.	Hearts (h and a)	4-0, 1-1
1918–19	Rd. F	v.	Hearts (h and a)	1-2, 0-1
1919–20	Rd. F	v.	Hearts (a)	1-1, 1-3
1920–21	Rd. S	v.	St. Bernards (h)	4-2
	F	v.	Hearts (a)	1-0

1921–22	Rd. S	v.	Hearts (h)	2-0
	F	v.	St. Bernards (h)	3-2
1922–23	Rd. S	v.	Leith Athletic (h)	4-0
	F	v.	Hearts (h)	1-1, 2-1
1923–24	Rd. S	v.	St. Bernards (a)	2-2, 5-1
	F	v.	Hearts (a)	1-1, 2-1
1924–25	Rd. S	v.	Hearts (a)	0-0, 1-0
	F	v.	Leith Athletic (h)	3-0
1925–26	Rd. S	v.	St. Bernards (h)	9-0
	F	v.	Hearts (a)	2-1
1926–27	Rd. S	v.	Leith Athletic (h)	3-1
	F	v.	Hearts (h)	1-5
1927–28	Rd. S	v.	St. Bernards (h)	7-1
	F	v.	Hearts (a)	2-2, 2-1
1928–29	Rd. S	v.	Leith Ath (h)	0-0, 0-0, 5-0
	F	v.	Hearts (h)	3-2
1929–30	Rd. S	v.	St. Bernards (a)	4-3
	F	v.	Hearts (a)	4-4, 1-1
	Hearts won 9-5 on corners			
1930–31	Rd. S	v.	Leith Athletic (h)	2-2, 3-0
	F	v.	Hearts (h)	4-5
1931–32	Rd. S	v.	St. Bernards (a)	0-3
1932–33	Rd. S	v.	Leith Athletic (h)	2-1
	F	v.	Hearts (a)	0-4
1933–34	Rd. S	v.	Leith Athletic (h)	2-2, 4-1
	F	v.	Hearts (a)	0-4
1934–35	Rd. S	v.	Leith Athletic (h)	3-0
	F	v.	Hearts (h)	4-2
1935–36	Rd. S	v.	St. Bernards (h)	1-1, 0-0, 2-3
1936–37	Rd. S	v.	St. Bernards (a)	1-0
	F	v.	Hearts (a)	2-6
1937–38	Rd. S	v.	Leith Athletic (a)	2-0
	F	v.	Hearts (h)	4-0
1938–39	Rd. S	v.	St. Bernards (h)	2-0
	F	v.	Hearts (a)	3-1
1939–40	Rd. S	v.	St. Bernards (a)	1-0
	F	v.	Hearts (h)	2-3
1940–41	*No competition: Hearts scratched*			
1941–42	Rd. S	v.	St. Bernards (h)	7-1
	F	v.	Hearts (a)	2-3

1942–43	Rd. F	v.	Hearts (h)	1-1, 3-2
1943–44	Rd. S	v.	Edinburgh City (h)	6-1
	F	v.	Hearts (a)	1-2
1944–45	Rd. S	v.	Edinburgh City (h)	5-3
	F	v.	Hearts (h)	3-1
1945–46	Rd. F	v.	Hearts (a)	2-3
1946–47	Rd. S	v.	Edinburgh City (a)	9-0
	F	v.	Hearts (h)	2-1
1947–48	Rd. F	v.	Hearts (a)	3-0
1948–49	Rd. S	v.	Leith Athletic (h)	4-0
	F	v.	Hearts (h)	2-1
1949–51	*No competition; fixtured too far behind*			
1951–52	Rd. F	v.	Hearts (a)	3-0
1952–53	Rd. F	v.	Hearts (h)	4-2
1953–54	Rd. F	v.	Hearts (a)	0-1
1954–55	Rd. F	v.	Hearts (h)	3-4
1955–56	Rd. F	v.	Hearts (a)	1-2
1956–57	Rd. F	v.	Hearts (h)	2-1
1957–58	Rd. F	v.	Hearts (a)	0-3
1958–59	Rd. F	v.	Hearts (h)	2-0
1959–60	Rd. F	v.	Hearts (a)	3-2
1960–61	Rd. F	v.	Hearts (h)	4-2
1961–62	Rd. F	v.	Hearts (a)	1-3
1962–63	Rd. F	v.	Hearts (h)	2-0
1963–64	Rd. F	v.	Hearts (a)	0-3
1964–65	Rd. F	v.	Hearts (h)	1-3
1965–66	Rd. F	v.	Hearts (a)	2-4
1966–67	Rd. F	v.	Hearts (h)	1-2
1967–68	Rd. F	v.	Hearts (a)	1-1, 1-0
1968–69	Rd. F	v.	Hearts (h)	1-2
1969–70	Rd. F	v.	Hearts (a)	2-3
1970–71	Rd. F	v.	Hearts (h)	1-0
1971–72	Rd. S	v.	Berwick Rangers (h)	4-1
	Final not played			
1972–73	*No competition*			
1973–74	*Hibs did not take part*			

1974–75	Rd. S	v.	Berwick Rangers (h)	3-0
	F	v.	Hearts (a)	1-2 aet
1975–76	*Hibs did not take part*			
1976–77	Rd. S	v.	Meadowbank Thistle (h)	4-1
	F	v.	Hearts (h)	1-0
1977–78	Rd. S	v.	Berwick Rangers (h)	4-0
	F	v.	Meadowbank Thistle (h)	4-0
1978–79	*No competition*			
1979–80	Rd. S	v.	Meadowbank Thistle (h)	3-1
	F	v.	Hearts (a)	2-2
	Hibs won on penalties			
1980–81	Rd. S	v.	Meadowbank Thistle	0-0
	Meadowbank won on penalties			
1981–82	Rd. S	v.	Hearts (h)	1-2
1982–83	Rd. S	v.	Meadowbank Thistle (h)	2-1
	F	v.	Berwick Rangers (a)	2-2
	Hibs won on penalties			
1983–84	Rd. S	v.	Meadowbank Thistle (h)	1-1
	Meadowbank won on penalties			
1984–85			*No competition*	
1985–86		v.	Hearts (h)	1-2
1986–87		v.	Hearts (a)	2-0
1987–88		v.	Hearts (h)	1-5
1988–89		v.	Hearts (a)	3-3; *lost pens*
1989–90		v.	Hearts (h)	0-0; *won pens*

Players Capped

Full International Appearances - Scotland

J. Blackley (7)	74 v CZ, ENG, BEL, ZAI; 76 v SWZ; 77 v WAL, SWE
D. Bremner (1)	76 v SWZ
B. Breslin (1)	97 v WAL
J. Brownlie (7)	71 v RUS; 72 v PER, NI, ENG; 73 v DEN (2); 76 v ROM
P. Callaghan (1)	00 v NI
J. Collins (4)	88 v SAR; 90 v EG, POL (sub), MAL
R. Combe (3)	48 v ENG, SWZ, BEL
P. Cormack (4)	66 v BRA; 69 v DEN; 70 v EIR, WG
A. Cropley (2)	72 v POR, BEL
A. Duncan (5)	75 v POR, WAL, NI, ENG, RUS
J. Dunn (5)	25 v WAL, NI; 27 v NI; 28 v NI, ENG
R. Glen (1)	00 v NI
A. Goram (3)	90 v EG, POL, MAL
J. Govan (6)	48 v ENG, WAL, BEL, SWZ, FR; 49 v NI
J. Grant (2)	59 v WAL, NI
A. Gray (1)	03 v NI
W. Groves (1)	88 v WAL
W. Hamilton (1)	65 v FIN
J. Harper (1)	76 v DEN
W. Harper (9)	23 v ENG, WAL, NI; 24 v ENG, WAL, NI; 25 v ENG, WAL, NI
H. Howie (1)	49 v WAL
R. Johnstone (13)	51 v ENG, DEN, FR; 52 v NI, ENG; 53 v ENG, SWE; 54 v WAL, ENG, NOR, FIN; 55 v NI, HUN
J. Kennedy (1)	97 v WAL
P. Kerr (1)	24 v NI
J. Lundie (1)	86 v WAL
W. McCartney (1)	02 v NI
J. McGhee (1)	86 v WAL
J. McLaren (1)	88 v WAL
J. Macleod (4)	61 v ENG, EIR (2), CZ
J. Main (1)	09 v NI
N. Martin (2)	65 v FIN, POL

P. Murray (2)	96 v NI; 97 v WAL
R. Neil (1)	96 v WAL
W. Ormond (6)	54 v ENG, NOR, FIN, AUS, URU; 59 v ENG
J. Pryce (1)	97 v WAL
L. Reilly (38)	49 v ENG, WAL, FR; 50 v WAL, NI, SWZ, FR; 51 v WAL, ENG, DEN, FR, BEL, AUS; 52 v NI, WAL, ENG, USA, DEN, SWE; 53 v ENG, WAL, NI, SWE; 54 v WAL; 55 v HUN (2), POR, YUG, AUS, ENG; 56 v ENG, WAL, NI, AUS; 57 v ENG, NI, WAL, YUG
H. Rennie (11)	01 v ENG; 02 v ENG, WAL, NI; 03 v ENG, WAL; 04 v NI; 05 v WAL; 06 v NI; 08 v NI, WAL
H. Ritchie (2)	23 v WAL; 28 V NI
W. Robb (1)	28 v WAL
A. Rough (2)	86 v WAL, ENG
E. Shaedler (1)	74 v WG
J. Scott (1)	66 v HOL
D. Shaw (8)	47 v WAL, NI; 48 v ENG, BEL, SWZ, FR; 49 v WAL, NI
G. Smith (18)	47 v ENG, NI; 48 v WAL, BEL, SWZ, FR; 52 v ENG, USA; 55 v POR, YUG, AUS, HUN; 56 v NI, WAL, ENG; 57 v SP (2) SWZ
P. Stanton (16)	66 v HOL; 69 v NI; 70 v EIR, AUS; 71 v DEN (2), POR, RUS, BEL; 72 v POR, BEL, HOL, WAL; 73 v WAL, NI; 74 v WG
G. Stewart (2)	06 v WAL, ENG
E. Turnbull (8)	48 v BEL, SWZ; 51 v AUS; 58 v HUN, POR, YUG, FR, PAR
D. Urquhart (1)	34 v WAL
T. Younger (8)	55 v POR, YUG, AUS, HUN; 56 v ENG, WAL, NI, AUS

England

J. Baker (5)	60 v YUG, SP, HUN, NI, SCO

Northern Ireland (previously Ireland)

P. Farrell (1)	38 v WAL
W. Gowdy (1)	36 v WAL
J. Jones (4)	36 v WAL; 37 v ENG, SCO, WAL
J. Parke (3)	64 v ENG, SP; 65 v SWZ

Wales

R. Atherton (2)	99 v NI, ENG

Eire

P. Farrell (2)   37 v SWZ, FR (see also Northern Ireland)
M. Gallagher (1)   54 v LUX

Under-23 Appearances - Scotland

J. Baxter (1)   59 v WAL
J. Blackley (4)   70 v FR, ENG, WAL; 71 v ENG
D. Bremner (3)   75 v ENG, WAL, SWE
J. Brownlie (2)   72 v ENG, WAL
P. Cormack (6)   65 v WAL, ENG; 67 v WAL, ENG; 68 v WAL, ENG
A. Cropley (3)   72 v WAL; 73 v ENG; 74 v WAL
A. Duncan (1)   71 v ENG
J. Easton (1)   64 v WAL
J. Harrower (1)   58 v NOR
N. Martin (1)   64 v FR
P. Marinello (2)   70 v FR, ENG
J. Macleod (2)   61 v ENG, Army
R. Nicol (2)   56 v ENG; 58 v NOR
J. Plenderleith (5)   57 v ENG; 58 v NOR (2), ENG; 60 v WAL
P. Stanton (3)   67 v WAL, ENG; 68 v ENG
C. Stein (1)   68 v ENG

England

J. Baker (5)   59 v POL, CZ; 60 v FR, NOR; 61 v IT

Under-21 Appearances - Scotland

A. Brazil (1)   78 v WAL
J. Collins (8)   88 v BEL, ENG, NOR; 89 v YUG, FR; 90 v YUG, FR,
                        NOR
B. Hamilton (2)   90 v FR, NOR
G. Hunter (3)   87 v EIR; 88 v BEL, ENG (sub)
A. McLeod (3)   79 v NOR (2), POR
E. May (2)   89 v YUG (sub), FR
L. Muir (1)   77 v CZ
C. Paterson (3)   81 v SWE, IT (2)
B. Rice (1)   85 v WG
P. Stanton (1)   77 v CZ
J. Tortolano (2)   87 v WG, EIR

Scottish League Appearances

J. Blackley (1)	72 v ENG
B. Breslin (4)	98 v ENG, NI; 99 v ENG; 00 v NI
D. Bremner (1)	76 v ENG
J. Brownlie (1)	72 v ENG
P. Callaghan (2)	00 v NI; 03 v NI
R. Combe (4)	49 v ENG, EIR; 54 v ENG, EIR
P. Cormack (6)	67 v ENG, EIR; 68 v NI; 69 v ENG; 70 v ENG, NI
J. Cuthbertson (1)	48 v ENG
A. Duncan (3)	71 v EIR; 73 v ENG; 76 v ENG
J. Dunn (1)	23 v NI
R. Glen (2)	00 v ENG, NI
J. Govan (1)	53 v EIR
J. Graham (1)	71 v EIR
J. Grant (6)	59 v ENG, NI, EIR; 60 v NI, EIR; 62 v EIR
A. Gray (1)	03 v ENG
W. Hamilton (1)	65 v ENG
W. Harper (3)	25 v ENG, IRE; 25 v ENG
R. Johnstone (6)	51 v EIR; 52 v ENG, NI; 53 v EIR, ENG; 54 v EIR
S. Kean (1)	47 v NI
J. Kennedy (1)	97 v NI
P. Kerr (2)	24 v NI; 27 v NI
A. Linwood (1)	49 v NI
W. McCartney (2)	02 v ENG; 03 v ENG
T. McFarlane (1)	97 v NI
W. McGinnigle (1)	25 v NI
A. McLeod (1)	80 v EIR
J. Macleod (1)	61 v ENG
J. McNamara (1)	80 v NI
J. Main (1)	08 v ENG
N. Martin (2)	64 v ENG; 65 v EIR
P. Murray (1)	97 v NI
R. Nutley (1)	40 v NI
W. Ormond (9)	47 v NI; 48 v NI; 49 v ENG; 50 v NI; 51 v ENG; 53 v EIR, NI; 54 v ENG; 58 v ENG
A. Raisbeck (1)	97 v NI
L. Reilly (13)	49 v NI; 50 v ENG, EIR; 51 v NI, EIR; 52 v ENG; 53 v ENG, EIR, NI; 56 v ENG, EIR, NI; 57 v EIR
H. Rennie (6)	01 v ENG; 03 v NI; 04 v ENG; 05 v ENG; 06 v ENG; 08 v ENG

H. Ritchie (5)	22 v NI; 23 v ENG, NI; 24 v NI; 27 v ENG
D. Shaw (2)	49 v NI, EIR
G. Smith (9)	48 v NI; 50 v ENG, EIR; 51 v ENG; 53 v EIR; 55 v ENG; 56 v ENG, EIR, NI
W. Smith (3)	12 v NI; 14 v ENG; 13 v STH LGE
P. Stanton (7)	66 v ENG; 68 v NI; 69 v EIR; 70 v ENG, NI; 71 v EIR; 73 v ENG
C. Stein (2)	68 v ENG; 69 v ENG
E. Stevenson (1)	70 v NI
G. Stewart (1)	06 v ENG
E. Turnbull (4)	49 v ENG; 51 v ENG; 53 v NI; 59 v ENG
W. Watson (1)	34 v NI
T. Younger (4)	56 v ENG, NI, EIR, DEN

'B' Internationals

T. McDonald (1)	54 v ENG
J. Mulkerrin (1)	56 v ENG
E. Turnbull (1)	56 v ENG

Wartime Internationals

R. Baxter (2)	Apr. 44 v ENG; Oct. 44 v ENG
T. Bogan (1)	Apr. 45 v ENG
M. Busby (2)	Oct. 41 v ENG; Apr. 42 v ENG
J. Caskie (5)	Oct. 41 v ENG; Jan. 42 v ENG; Feb. 44 v ENG; Apr. 44 v ENG; Oct. 44 v ENG
S. Kean (1)	Apr. 43 v ENG
A. Milne (1)	Oct. 44 v ENG
D. Shaw (2)	Apr. 46 v ENG; May 46 v SWZ
G. Smith (2)	Oct. 44 v ENG; Jan 46 v BEL

R. Baxter, M. Busby and J. Caskie are sometimes listed with Middlesbrough, Liverpool and Everton respectively, the clubs with whom they were registered at the outbreak of war. The above caps were won while they were regular members of the Hibs' team and would otherwise have been playing for Hibs.

The following abbreviations have been used (except for League Internationals)

ALB	Albania	NOR	Norway
AUS	Austria	PAR	Paraguay
BEL	Belgium	PER	Peru
BRA	Brazil	POL	Poland
CZ	Czechoslovakia	POR	Portugal
DEN	Denmark	ROM	Romania
EG	East Germany	RUS	Russia
EIR	Republic of Ireland	SAR	Saudi Arabia
ENG	England	SCO	Scotland
FIN	Finland	SP	Spain
FR	France	SWE	Sweden
HOL	Holland	SWZ	Switzerland
HUN	Hungary	URU	Uruguay
ICE	Iceland	USA	United States
IT	Italy	WAL	Wales
LUX	Luxembourg	WG	West Germany
MAL	Malta	YUG	Yugoslavia
NI	Northern Ireland (see below)	ZAI	Zaire

Note: Northern Ireland. Ireland was divided into Northern Ireland and the Republic of Ireland in 1922, and therefore up to then there was only one international team representing the whole island. From 1922 until about 1954, Northern Ireland included Republic players in British Championship matches only, the two parts of Ireland fielding separate sides against other opponents. Since 1954, only Northern Irish players have represented Northern Ireland in the British Championship or elsewhere. In this book, NI has been used to represent the combined Irish teams that played in the British Championship up to 1954 and also the Northern Ireland teams since 1922, while EIR represents teams exclusively from the Republic of Ireland.

For League Internationals, the abbreviations designate the opposing country rather than the league itself as follows:

DEN	Danish League
EIR	League of Ireland
ENG	Football League
NI	Irish League
STH LGE	(English) Southern League

Index

Index